Living as God's Holy People

Living as God's Holy People: Holiness and Community in Paul

The 2008 Didsbury Lectures

Kent Brower

Paternoster:
thinking faith

16 15 14 13 12 11 10   7 6 5 4 3 2 1

First published 2010 by Paternoster
Paternoster is an imprint of Authentic Media Limited
Milton Keynes
www.authenticmedia.co.uk

British Library Cataloguing in Publication Data

A catalogue record for this book is available from the
British Library

ISBN-13: 978-1-84227-667-9

Cover design by David McNeill

Printed and bound in the UK by Bell & Bain Ltd., Glasgow

To Francine, with deepest love and unending admiration.

You have been my companion on the journey for decades. Your life of faithfulness to God and in service to others, primarily through special needs education, has reflected the love of God poured out in your heart through the Spirit.

Table of Contents

Abbreviations   ix

Preface   xi

Chapter One: Paul and Holiness   1
  1 Paul, the Jewish Apostle to the Gentiles   1
  2 Holiness in the Light of Christ   4
  3 The Righteousness of God Revealed   6
  4 The Human Condition   14
  5 Peace with God   22

Chapter Two: Holiness and the Holy Spirit   26
  1 Life in the Spirit   26
  2 Paul's View of Humanity   30
  3 Walking According to the Spirit, Not According   33
    to the Flesh
  4 The Mind Set on the Spirit, Not on the Flesh   37
  5 The Witness of the Spirit   42
  6 Sanctified by the Spirit   45
  7 The Fruit of the Spirit   47
  8 The Gifts of the Spirit   50

Chapter Three: Holiness and Community in Corinth   56
  1 Status, Sex and Temple   56
  2 The Temple of the Holy Spirit   61
  3 Worship in Community: Discerning the Body   66
  4 Saints and Sinners in Community   80

Chapter Four: Holiness in the Real World   **86**
  1 Holiness and the New Creation   86
  2 Holiness, Identity and Citizenship   95
  3 Holiness and Eschatology   100
  4 Contagious Holiness   105

Select Bibliography   108

Notes   118

Abbreviations

AB	Anchor Bible
BNTC	Black's New Testament Commentaries
ICC	International Christian Commentary
JBL	*Journal of Biblical Literature*
JSNT	*Journal for the Study of the New Testament*
JSNTSS	Journal for the Study of the New Testament: Supplement Series
NCB	New Century Bible
NICNT	New International Commentary on the New Testament
NovTS	Novum Testamentum Supplements
NTS	*New Testament Studies*
NTT	New Testament Theology
SBT	*Studies in Biblical Theology*
SNTSMS	Society of New Testament Studies, Monograph Series
SNTW	Studies of the New Testament and its World
WBC	Word Biblical Commentary
WThJ	*Wesleyan Theological Journal*
WUNT	*Wissenschaftliche Untersuchungen zum Neuen Testament*

Preface

When I received the invitation from Nazarene Theological College, Manchester, to deliver the thirtieth in the series of Didsbury Lectures, I was honoured and humbled. In accepting the invitation, I could not help but reflect back over the years of these lectures. I especially cast my mind back to the inaugural series delivered by Professor F. F. Bruce in 1979. He addressed himself to *Men and Movements in the Early Church: Studies in Early Non-Pauline Christianity* (1979). It is, therefore, a double honour – and not a little intimidating – to follow in his footsteps in this series, not least because he was my PhD supervisor.

Professor Bruce's expertise ran widely in biblical studies: Hebrew Bible, Second Temple-period literature and New Testament. Pauline studies were a particular focus of his attention. When I was writing a short commentary on the Thessalonian Epistles, I had frequent occasion to turn to Professor Bruce's excellent commentary in the Word Biblical Commentary series and benefited greatly from it. But what particularly struck me then was the way he understood Paul's call to his Thessalonian readers to live holy lives in readiness for the Parousia. His views on this aspect of Paul's epistles, and so much else in Paul, encourage me to think that he would find some things in this series with which to agree. In turn, I hope that this series will, in some very small way, be a tribute to the memory of Professor Bruce and his own immense contribution to the lives of so many around the world.

The question of how Paul addresses the issue of purity (and holiness) in light of his roots in the Second Temple period is now of considerable interest in the scholarly world. This emphasis is due, at least in part, to the renewed recognition that Paul was a Jew and therefore he needs to be understood in the context of the intersection of Second Temple period Judaism with the Graeco-Roman world. His encounter with the risen and ascended Christ leads Paul to the re-reading of his own context, including his scriptures, in the light of Christ. The conviction that God has now acted decisively in the story of Israel through the sending of his son Jesus as messiah fundamentally re-shapes his thinking and practice. This is now the age to come, as shown by the untimely resurrection of Jesus from the dead and the manifest presence of the Spirit in the new community of believers in Jesus Messiah.

Paul sees himself as called by God to carry the good news of God's action in Christ to the Gentiles as part of the fulfilment of God's purposes for his entire created order. Paul's own explicit self-understanding is set out in Romans 15:15–20. He has been commissioned by God *to be a minister of Christ Jesus to the Gentiles in the priestly service of the gospel of God, so that the offering of the Gentiles may be acceptable, sanctified by the Holy Spirit*. Paul then epitomizes his mission in these terms: *to win obedience from the Gentiles*.

The bedrock of Paul's identity as a Jew is God's call to Israel: they are called to be his people and therefore to be holy as God is holy. But this call to be a kingdom of priests and a holy nation has now been extended to the Gentiles. The reason for God's call of the Gentiles, Paul believes, is that they are to join God's people in the proclamation of the good news of salvation to all. Paul sees this as the creation of a new people gathered from the righteous remnant of Israel, that is, those who are followers of Jesus Messiah, and those Gentiles who respond to the procla-mation of the good news. Together they are fashioned into a renewal of God's holy people, created by the Spirit and centred on Jesus, who is the representative and embodiment of Israel. This is a new configuration without regard to ethnicity. The new people of God, like Paul himself, are to be agents of that recon-ciliation offered to all in and through Christ.

The question of how God's new holy people are to live according to Paul is the concern of this book. Throughout his epistles – occasional letters to scattered congregations throughout the eastern Mediterranean, and to Rome itself – Paul addresses this question. He is fully aware of the situation in which the recipients of the letters live their lives. But his conviction is that the call to be God's holy people is not restricted to ethnic Israel but encompasses all, Jews and Gentiles, who follow Jesus Messiah. This conviction means that his people would often find themselves living in a counter-cultural fashion.

Paul builds upon his view of this call – that the call to be a holy people extends to all who follow Jesus. In Paul's view, this new people of God is to embody the holiness of God wherever they live just as Israel was to embody it. But how does this work out in practice? Far from being an addendum to his theology, the question of how they are to live as God's holy people is a central concern in all of Paul's epistles.

Paul would not recognize a theology–practice division, as if theology and practice do not connect. Nor, for that matter, would he recognize the all-too-often caricatured division of 'academic v. practical'. Paul's theology, like his grand vision of God's purposes, is all-encompassing. His ethics is always theological ethics; his theology is always practical theology. His theology is not merely propositional or theoretical as if one could isolate justification by faith alone from the consequences of that new relationship with God in the life of the holy community. Thus, sanctification and justification are not separated in Paul's thought as if a right relationship with God could fail to issue in holy living. Nor does Paul focus primarily on the sanctification of justified individuals. God's people are holy together in Christ through the Spirit.

Some of these issues are addressed in chapter one. An outline of Paul's view of the righteousness of God and the human condition sets the stage for a description of the solution to the alienation of the human condition that God has offered in Christ. In the gospel, Paul argues that God's faithfulness not only to Israel but to the entire created order is fulfilled in and through the obedience of Jesus, Son of David, Son of God. Because of this obedience, we have peace with God.

In chapter two, the place of the Holy Spirit in holy living is discussed by using some of Paul's descriptions of life in the Spirit. Those who do not have the Spirit are not Christ's, according to Paul. Those who are in Christ walk according to the Spirit with a mind set on the Spirit. The Spirit, in turn, bears witness with their spirits to their participation in the people of God. God's holy people manifest the fruit of the Spirit in their lives and exercise the gifts of the Spirit given to them for the health of the community and the witness of the people of God.

If a biblical test-case for living as God's holy people in community within the Graeco–Roman context were needed, no better place could be found than Corinth. Chapter three looks in particular at 1 Corinthians – to a context that some scholars think bears an uncanny resemblance to the twenty-first century in postmodern (and post-Christian) Western Europe and North America. In this context, the issues of purity and defilement, seen especially against the backdrop of inappropriate sexual expression and idol worship, are crucial if the people of God are to be God's holy temple and worship the holy God.

Chapter Four focuses on the contagion of holy living. Contagious holiness is discussed particularly in the connection between holy living and Paul's new creation language. That kind of language invites exploration of its implications in terms of environmental relations as well as in personal and communal terms. Inevitably, a reflection on issues like the environment leads to further consideration of the already/not yet tension of the existence of God's holy people. The thorny questions remain. What are the implications of their identity as citizens of heaven while they live as people in the matrix of human life? How are they to display their identity? Paul rejects any suggestion that the people ought to be isolated from the surrounding culture. Rather, Paul challenges the holy people to live prophetic lives in their societies. Their holiness is to be contagious in a context where sin is also contagious, but one in which the tension of the already but not yet of the life of holiness is never forgotten.

This short book is substantially the same as the Didsbury Lectures delivered at Nazarene Theological College in October 2008. These, in turn, were based on an earlier version delivered as the Wiley Lectures at Point Loma Nazarene University in February 2006. Comments and critiques at both institutions have influenced this version of the lectures. Nevertheless, the temptation to make the book significantly longer and therefore a better account of Paul's challenge to holy living has been resisted. Thus, the book bears a very close resemblance to the lectures delivered in Manchester and, to a lesser extent, in San Diego, but this time with full footnotes and bibliography.

The most important help in developing the ideas in the lectures has been the dialogue with my colleagues at NTC, PLNU and Nazarene Theological Seminary, as well as my MA and PhD students in Manchester. All have influenced me in a great many ways. Their contribution has been added to the wide range of scholars who have guided my thinking over the years. I hope that I have given them appropriate credit in the book's footnotes and bibliography, but almost inevitably I have many debts of which I am not even conscious. Of course, any errors or shortcomings remain mine.

Kent Brower
Christmas 2008

Chapter One

Paul and Holiness

1 Paul, the Jewish Apostle to the Gentiles

Holiness is a central concern of Paul's throughout his entire life and ministry before and after his encounter with the risen and ascended Christ.

At first glance this statement seems odd or eccentric. But further reflection shows that this is not as far from the mark as might first be supposed. In some of his clearest autobiographical material, when Paul describes his life before he is apprehended by the risen Lord, he notes that *as to the law, [he was] a Pharisee. As to righteousness under the law [he was] blameless* (Phil. 3:5–6).[1] Paul becomes obsessed with following the risen Christ, but we really cannot understand Paul's thinking and actions without constant reference to his Pharisaic roots.

As is now commonly recognized, the Pharisees were one of the holiness movements in the Second Temple Period. The quest for holiness dominated the religious thought of the period to the extent that religious conflict within Judaism often centred on what it meant to be and to become God's holy people.[2] Indeed, much of the conflict between Jesus and the Pharisees can best be understood in this context. Even the relationship between defilement and sin during this period was the subject of sectarian debate.[3] For the Pharisees and Saul, their self-professed star adherent (see Gal. 1:14), the quest for holiness included extending the purity that the Torah required of priests in the temple to the entire land of Israel.

There is considerable debate about whether purity was connected *only* to the temple during the Second Temple period or
whether it was widely practiced in general. John Poirier argues
that purity was an issue that extended well beyond specific
temple purity. He notes that the archaeological evidence for the
existence of *'miqva'ot* with the remains of pre-70 Palestinian
synagogues strongly suggests that 'one could not enter [syna-
gogue] without taking care of one's own purity status.'[4] If the
people of Israel were a kingdom of priests and a holy nation,
and if the holy God were ever to make his dwelling again in
their midst, then it followed that purity must be maintained at a
higher level than had heretofore been the case. Purity issues,
then, would have been paramount for the Pharisaic Paul. At the
heart of questions of holiness and purity in Second Temple
Pharisaism lies the appropriate practice in table fellowship.[5]
Although the issue is not simply ritual purity, table fellowship
as a symbol of the unity of the community is at the core of a vig-
orous dispute between Paul and his fellow apostles (see Gal. 2).

This concern for observance sounds to modern Gentile ears
like legalism. No doubt some Pharisees did observe Torah as an
external code – holiness people, then and now, can easily drift
into legalism. As Schreiner observes, 'the Moasaic covenant
was not intrinsically legalistic, but was instead a nationalistic
covenant.'[6] But despite what might appear to be a legalistic and
external approach by some of them,[7] purity was never just a
matter of externals. The evidence from the Qumran community,
the radical holiness separationist group that flourished
throughout much of the late Second Temple period, reminds us
that their understanding of purity includes the fact that out-
ward purity must be matched by inward purity.[8]

It would be surprising, then, and an indication of just how
much we have obscured the real Paul, if it were thought that the
language of holiness, purity and obedience had been jettisoned
by Paul. Yet the reason for this is not particularly hard to find.
The anxiety, especially strong among Protestants, to distance
Paul from any sort of 'salvation by works' risks distorting
Paul's gospel, by separating sanctification from justification,

holy living from holy status, ethics from theology, practice from theory. The issue of faith versus works may well be significant for Christian identity against the backdrop of the later Pelagian controversy and the still later Reformation but this is not Paul's issue. Indeed, 'the Pauline theme of obedience should not be identified as a new legalism, for the new obedience is the work of the Spirit in those who are the new creation work of Christ.'[9] We need to be careful that the 'salvation by works' fear does not skew the discussion so that obedience and ethics are at risk of disappearing beneath a wave of anxiety that finds even the phrase 'grace-enabled obedience' to be suspect.[10]

Paul is the Jewish apostle to the Gentiles, wrestling with the significance to his ancestral faith of his encounter with the crucified and risen Messiah, on the one hand, and to the evident work of God through the Spirit among the Gentiles, on the other. The action of God in Christ is the beginning of a complete re-casting of his own understanding, including his view of holiness. But Paul remains a Jew in his orientation.[11] Recent scholars have drawn particular attention to the fact that a major feature of Paul's work is to remind his Gentile readers that they are part of the people of God by adoption into the covenant that God has established with Israel.[12] But it is a new covenant. Precisely what its relationship is to the 'old' covenant is the subject of debate. As Hafemann notes, 'scripture testifies to one, constant relationship between God and his people throughout redemptive history that is formalized and embodied in the successive covenants.'[13] The key point is that Paul does not convert from Judaism to Christianity so much as re-shape his whole perspective on his ancestral faith in the light of Christ.

Paul also remains fundamentally committed to 'the biblical and ancient Jewish notion of moral purity'.[14] The point is crucial. Holiness and ethics are not synonymous, of course, but 'a holy people is still best characterized by their way of being and their manner of behaving.'[15] Paul's gospel is being proclaimed in a Graeco-Roman context in which moral purity is not central either to worship or public life. But neither does Paul reduce the gospel to an imposition of a new code of ethics. As Gorman notes, he 'offers a radically new interpretation of holiness molded by the gospel of the Messiah who was crucified by Rome but raised and exalted by God'.[16] The community of God's holy people is created through the death and resurrection of Christ and its entire existence is shaped by it. All of the life of the believing community is transformed by the presence of the risen Christ. Paul's concern with holy living, then, does not end with his encounter with the risen Christ. Rather it is an essential ingredient in his entire understanding of God's big purposes and the place of his people in them. God still calls his people to be holy.

2 Holiness in the Light of Christ

For Paul the gospel of God is the starting point for understanding the holy life. This is seen clearly in Romans. Paul starts his discussion with *the gospel of God ... concerning his Son* which is *the power of God for salvation* and in which the *righteousness of God is revealed* (Rom. 1:1–17). Paul and his readers share basic theological presuppositions. At the same time the contingent demands of Paul's discussion even in Romans are important to note.[17] They are those who know and worship the holy God. On that basis, Paul sets out the gospel of God.

Paul's language here is instructive. The Gospel is not a series of propositions or a body of belief. Rather it is the good news concerning God's son. The content, the whole thrust of the Gospel, is none other than Jesus himself – hence Christ dominates Paul's thinking. This is seen in his repeated use of the highly significant phrase 'in Christ', as the location and identity of the people of God. Indeed, as David Stubbs notes, Paul's overall theological vision includes 'a christologically centred understanding of the *pistis Christou* passages ... and the centring of soteriology around the concept of 'participation in Christ'.[18] Participation in Christ is the focus of the whole story. In Christ, God has acted decisively, supremely seen in the resurrection. As N. T. Wright states, '*What the creator/covenant god was supposed to do for Israel at the end of history, this god had done for Jesus in the middle of history.*[19] The turning point of the ages has arrived[20] and God's ultimate good purposes are already affecting the present, albeit in anticipatory fashion.[21] In fact, as Paul already knows, Christ alone gives coherence to the whole story of God's dealing with his covenant people.[22]

But questions arise related to the actual effect of the gospel. Why is God through Christ welcoming the Gentiles into his covenant people? And on what terms? And what about the promises to Israel? Has God simply abrogated them? Of course, Paul has a variety of reasons for writing Romans. But included among them must have been some attempt to address these very real questions which his gospel was raising with respect to his ancestral faith (see especially Romans 9—11).[23] Critically, what does it mean to live as God's holy people, no longer defined primarily in ethnic terms, in the midst of a world that takes a pluralistic approach to religious practice and which is essentially hostile to God?[24] Although all of these questions are interrelated, it is this latter question to which this series is directed in particular: what does it mean to be and to live as God's holy people?

In Romans, Paul enters into a sustained theological discussion in response to it. His strategy seems to be to restate his gospel, God's solution offered in Christ to the human condition. By appeal to the story of Israel, Paul hopes to show the validity of his gospel. In the first instance, Paul argues, although 'God called Abraham to deal with the problem of Adam',[25] Israel became part of the problem, as the history of his own people amply demonstrates. Nevertheless, God is faithful to his promises. But how? Answer – they all come to their focus in Christ, the goal to which the law and the prophets always pointed (1:4; 3:21–26; 10:4; 16:25–27). Furthermore, despite present evidence to the contrary (see 9—11), he confidently affirms that, however mysterious or unexpected the way might be, God will also redeem Israel (11:26–30) and thereby bring his salvation offered in Christ to fulfilment, to Jew first and also to the Gentiles (1:16–17).

Paul reminds his readers that he has been *set apart for the gospel of God … to bring about the obedience of faith … among all the nations* (Rom. 1:1–6). When he sums up his ministry in Romans 15, he writes about the grace given to him *to be a minister of Christ Jesus to the Gentiles in the priestly service of the gospel of God, so that the offering of the Gentiles may be acceptable, sanctified by the Holy Spirit … In Christ Jesus, then, I have reason to be proud of my work for God … what Christ has wrought through me to win obedience from the Gentiles, by word and deed, by the power of signs and wonders, by the power of the Spirit of God* (Rom. 15:17–19).[26] Clearly, then, for Paul his theological reflections are not cut off from the question of how God's holy people are to live.

Two key phrases are *sanctified [or made holy] by the Holy Spirit* and *obedience of faith*. Here is language that Paul uses to describe his mission and purpose. This is addressed by Paul in a surprising number of places. Almost certainly it has to do with living as God's holy people. Aspects of this will be discussed in the next three chapters. But first, we need to give a brief sketch of Paul's understanding of the gospel as expressed in the important phrase 'righteousness of God'.

3 The Righteousness of God Revealed

At the heart of Paul's gospel stands his understanding of the righteousness of God.[27] But this simple phrase is fraught with complexity. Does it have essentially a forensic meaning[28] and, if so, is that better understood in terms of guilt and acquittal set in Roman jurisprudence or is it to be anchored in the OT notion of righteousness and justice?

A recent significant study by Andrie B. du Toit argues just this point. But du Toit admits that the forensic metaphor has its limitations since it can only depict sin as guilt before God. 'It also cannot describe the specific effect of Christ's salvific work. For that purpose, Paul had to resort to other metaphors like deliverance (Rom. 3:24), atonement (3:25) and reconciliation (5:10–11). An additional weakness is that, apart from their new status as *dikaioi* and the imperative resulting from it, the forensic imagery focuses pre-eminently on believers' *entry* into the new community. It reveals very little about the nature of their new life in Christ.'[29]

The explanation of the 'righteousness of God' itself could occupy an entire series. Judging from some of the recent discussion, whether such a debate would add more light than heat might be open to question. For our reading of Paul, the approach taken by N. T. Wright and others in the so-called 'New Perspective' understands Paul better and therefore offers much more fruit than some of the older reading.[30] For our more modest purposes several summary points on the righteousness of God may be useful.

First, the righteousness of God is primarily the redeeming and saving activity of God. Many scholars now agree with John Ziesler[31] that 'the verb "justify" is used relationally, often with the forensic meaning "acquit", but that the noun [*dikaiosunē*], and the adjective δικαῖος have behavioural meanings.'[32] But even when the forensic sense is present, the words 'are forensic in the Hebrew sense, i.e., they represent restoration of the community or covenant relationship'.[33] It is therefore primarily a description of God's power in action, rescuing and judging. Paul now believes that 'God is revealing his own covenant faithfulness through the gospel, which is the world-changing event of God's power for salvation, the death and resurrection of Jesus Christ.'[34]

Second, the righteousness of God is best understood in the context of God's faithfulness. This faithfulness is to his created order in general and to his covenant people in particular.[35] A key concern of Paul's is to show God's righteousness in his faithfulness in sustaining his own covenant relationship with Israel despite her failure. Thus, N T Wright states that 'this divine righteousness always was, and remained throughout the relevant Jewish literature, the *covenant faithfulness of God.'[36]

But the adequacy of covenant faithfulness to sum up Paul's conceptual heritage has recently been criticised.[37] God's faithfulness does not start with covenant relationships. While

Reformed theologians usually start from the premise that any relationship involving God is covenantal in character,[38] Paul Williamson shows that 'the biblical order is relationship, then covenant; rather than covenant, hence relationship.'[39] This is clearly significant for our purposes. As Williamson notes, God's redemptive activity 'is concerned not merely with the restoration of the divine-human relationship established at creation, but ultimately with the renewal of all things, including creation itself ... It is towards this eschatological objective that each of the divine-human covenants in Scripture advances. The glue that binds all the biblical covenants together is God's creative purpose of universal blessing.'[40]

Covenant faithfulness, then, is a part of God's faithfulness to his entire created order. The reason for God's faithfulness is profoundly simple: in John's language, *God so loved the world*. God is faithful to all of his creation right from the opening chapters of Genesis in primeval history, not just from his call of Abram in Genesis 12:1. Or, to put it another way, 'God's eschatological redemptive action for Israel is seen within the context of God's salvific act for all creation.'[41] This faithfulness, in the grand narrative of scripture, leads to the call of Abram, the redemptive action of rescuing Israel from Egypt and the establishment of covenants with them. It carries on through the monarchy to the exile and return. And it comes to fullness, in Paul's view, in that supreme demonstration of God's faithfulness in the sending of the son.

Third, the righteousness of God is also seen in his activity as judge. Judgement occurs 'because of the prevalence of oppression and injustice in the world, and because of underlying notions of the goodness of the proper created order'.[42] Things are not as they should be. Paul concedes that persistent and ultimate opposition to the good purposes of God lead to punishment (see 2 Thess. 1:6–10). Thus, a comprehensive view of God's righteousness must include the notion of his righteous judgement in sovereign love over the created order. And, as Maru Nwachukwu reminds us, 'God's holiness is a fundamental aspect of his sovereignty.'[43] If the righteousness of God is understood only in terms of covenant faithfulness, inadequate attention is paid to the loving sovereignty of God over his creation. Covenant faithfulness is thus a subset of relational righteousness.

Here a word needs to be said about the law court connotations of righteousness. The notion of justice through the law court that appeases God as plaintiff is still popular. Andrew Lincoln thinks that 'the imagery of the law court predominates through the language of Justification. God's righteousness is the power by which those unable to be justified on the criterion of works are set right with him and being set in a right relationship with God involves his judicial verdict of pardon.'[44] On the fringes of this view is the idea of appeasing the angry God. But some recent discussions call aspects of this into question. Stuhlmacher, for instance, notes that

> although the doctrinal tradition of the church continues up to the present time to speaks of the appeasing of an angry God through the blood of Christ, or also of a satisfaction which takes place by means of Jesus' sacrificial death toward the God who has been injured in regard to his majesty through sin, there is no talk at all of this in the apostle's texts concerning atonement-reconciliation.[45]

Thus, in so far as the metaphor is legal, it has to do predominately with restorative justice, renewed participation in the covenant or vindication of the people against the enemies of God. The context of the law court is covenant law, covenant community and the covenant-making God. This means that redemption cannot be reduced to a legal transaction of a private nature between the individual and God. Snodgrass comments, 'one is not merely declared righteous; rather one is transformed by encounter with the powerful God who places people in right relation to himself.'[46] The righteousness of God therefore has less to do with pronouncing a dispassionate legal status than deliverance from the dominion of sin and restored relationship with God. But even when temporal judgement is involved, the goal is reconciling and corrective rather than punitive

judgement. God's righteousness as manifest in Christ is primarily a saving activity seen in the life and death and resurrection of
Jesus Christ through which the powers were defeated and new
life was bestowed.[47]

Fourth, this righteousness of God is seen most clearly in the
faithfulness of Christ. In recent years, a significant number of
Pauline scholars have accepted that Paul's *pistos christou* language refers fundamentally to the faithfulness of Christ.[48] Thus
the faithfulness of Christ as the obedient son is the means by
which God is faithful to his covenant promises. As Paul interprets his ancestral faith in the light of Christ, the obedient son
is the one on whom the focus of God's purposes for Israel
comes to rest. He is the fulfilment of the Torah. Jesus' coming in
the flesh and being crucified as the representative human and
the messiah is that all the good purposes of God come to focus
on Jesus, and hence, on Israel. According to Wright, 'Jesus, as
last Adam, had revealed what God's saving plan for the world
had really been – what Israel's vocation really had been – by
enacting it, becoming obedient to death, even the death of the
cross.'[49]

The faithfulness of Christ as the obedient son is central to
Paul's gospel. The obedience of the son is the means by which
God is faithful to his covenant promises. As Paul interprets his
ancestral faith in the light of Christ, the obedient son is the one
on whom the focus of God's purposes for Israel comes to rest.
He is the fulfilment of the Torah. The whole point of Jesus'
coming in the flesh and being crucified as the representative
human, the last Adam, and the Messiah of Israel is that all
the good purposes of God come to focus on Jesus, and hence,
on Israel. According to Wright, 'Jesus, as last Adam, had
revealed what God's saving plan for the world had really been –
what Israel's vocation really had been – by enacting it, becoming obedient to death, even the death of the cross.'[50]

Fifth, God's righteousness expressed in his covenant faithfulness was never just about Israel. God's big purposes in
calling Abraham and rescuing Israel were that his people would
be his redemptive agents to the whole world. This is not a

surprise to Paul. God has always acted righteously and now by justifying the ungodly (Rom. 3:21–26), he is acting according to his big purposes.[51] Thus, 'the covenantal idea itself *always included in principle* the belief that when the creator/covenant god acted on behalf of Israel, this would have a direct relation to the fate of the whole world, to the rooting out of evil and injustice from the whole creation.'[52] Paul has clear reasons for this. God's purpose is to redeem all of humanity, both Jews and Greeks, who together would become the agents of his good purposes in his world. The solution on offer is a universal one.

This is really demanded of Paul's whole argument. Those who argue that Paul does not proclaim a gospel that is universally effective do not grasp fully either Paul's narrative or the inner logic of his theology. Paul is equally clear, of course, that not all individuals accept this good news – his agonised discussion in Romans 9—11 echoes the lament of the Old Testament prophets. But the postulation of a limited atonement based upon God's eternal predestination of the elect represents the triumph of cold logic over the inner narrative of the text. Paul elaborates on this solution in terms of the problem, that is, the superabundance of God's grace in Christ being manifested by putting right what was wrong in Adam and thereby advancing the promise of God to Abraham through Christ (Rom. 4).

The point is made forcefully in Paul's very important passage in Romans 8:3–4: *God, by sending his own Son in the likeness of sinful flesh, and to deal with sin, condemned sin in the flesh, so that the just requirement of the law might be fulfilled in us, who walk not according to the flesh but according to the Spirit.* In the life, death and resurrection of Christ Jesus, God has dealt with the power of sin. In a powerful description that admirably sums up Paul's thought leading to this climatic statement, Wright explains that 'God's purpose, in and through all of this – in giving the Torah with this strange intention – was that sin might be drawn together, heaped up, not just in Israel in general but *upon Israel's true representative, the Messiah,* in order that it might there be dealt with, be condemned, once and for all.'[53] Wright continues,

For Paul, what was at stake was not simply God's judicial honor, in some Anselmic sense, but the mysterious power called sin, at large and destructive within God's world, needing to be brought to book, to have sentence passed and executed upon it, so that with its power broken, God could then give the life sin would otherwise prevent. That is what happened on the cross.[54]

Sixth, righteousness – when applied to God's activity towards his people – involves transformation. When used in its passive form, according to Sanders the verb *dikaioō* almost always means 'to be *changed,* to be transferred from one realm to another: from sin to obedience, from death to life, from being under law to being under grace. The verb is essentially a transfer term.'[55] This is expressed by Paul as a transfer of obedience from the service of sin and unrighteousness, to the service of righteousness, which Paul equates with being servants of God (Rom. 6:17–22). This is the context in which those who are in this relationship are being transformed. In this new relationship, the sphere of God's righteousness, God's active power affects those in its sphere and 'when human beings are drawn into its power, they begin to act as they should, as his covenant people.'[56]

Thus, any notion of distinguishing an imputed from an imparted righteousness is completely alien to Paul. As Wright notes, 'an older flattening out of these nuances into the either/ or of "forensic" and "ethical" meanings simply fails to catch what Paul is talking about.'[57] Righteousness is not a possession. It is a dynamic state, the fruit of a continued, in-faith, dynamic relationship begun and continued in faith. Human obedience is the means by which God's redemptive activity manifests itself. 'Our vocation is to embody the message of reconciliation by *becoming* the righteousness of God (δικαιοσύνη θεοῦ). That is to say, the vocation of the redeemed and transformed community is to become a visible manifestation of God's reconciling covenant love in the world.'[58] No relationship, no righteousness.

Finally, God's righteousness when humans are brought into its sphere is displayed by humans as a dynamic, relational way of being. Humans are not given a piece of God's righteousness, as if righteousness were a static thing in itself. To be sure, Paul can use gift language in association with righteousness (see Rom. 6:23), but righteousness itself is not a gift, a package, that God either imputes or imparts to people. Hence, as Stuhlmacher observes, 'the dogmatic distinction ... between a justification which is first only reckoned legally (forensic-imputed) and a justification which is creatively at work (effective) is ... an unbiblical distinction'.[59] Rather, people are righteous only in relationship to God.[60] Thus any attempt to distinguish an imputed from an imparted righteousness is completely alien to Paul.[61] This new reality is a relational reality, possible only in it and enduring only while in it. This is important to note. While transformation and new creation are the consequence of a right relationship, a new status, this new creation is always a new creation 'in Christ'.

God's righteous activity, therefore, cannot be exhausted by a purely forensic declaration that a human has righteous status. This is no legal fiction. Rather, the righteous activity of God directed to his people leads to the effective creation of a new reality through God. Although Schreiner abandoned his earlier view that righteousness is essentially transfer language in favour of a forensic view, he still argues that 'Paul never confines the gospel to the idea that we have been declared righteous before God. To be declared righteous without living righteously would be a monstrosity and an impossibility.'[62] At the same time, he wants to maintain the traditional view that 'Martin Luther was correct in emphasizing that we remain sinners ... [G]iven the already-but-not-yet character of Pauline eschatology, we are still stained with sin until the day we die. Luther was on target; we are justified but at the same time we are also sinners.'[63] But others disagree. In Paul's view, as Nwachukwu notes, 'the death of Jesus does not simply appease God's wrath ... but actualises an objective transformation in human beings.'[64] For Paul a restored relationship with a holy God in which there is no transformation of loyalty and behaviour, and no new creation is a non sequitur.

4 The Human Condition[65]

Living the holy life has to be seen against the context of the human condition. And apart from Christ, it is bleak.[66] In Romans 1:19 – 3:20, Paul draws the conclusions that 'all, both Jews and Greeks, are under the power of sin' (3:9). Paul defends this indictment by focusing initially upon the Gentile world. But human alienation is not peculiar to Gentiles. Not only does the story of alienation start from the beginning of the human story; membership in ethnic Israel does not exempt them from the human plight (Rom. 2).

What has happened to reach this sorry state? Three preliminary points need to be made. First, Paul never explains the *origin* of sin but he is quite clear that sinfulness is not the *natural* state of humanity. Second, God is not the origin of human folly nor is there a design fault in creation. Third, God has continued to reveal himself: creation itself points to the eternal power and divine nature of the creator God who, though invisible, reveals himself in his creation. This theme, of course, is a recurrent one in the Old Testament, most notably in the Psalms. As Lincoln observes, 'whereas Wisdom talks of a failure in natural theology, not having succeeded in reasoning from the creation to the Creator, Paul talks of a failure to respond to natural revelation, suppressing a knowledge of God that has already been given.'[67]

The primary description of the human condition is one of marred relationships and alienation. According to Paul, God's wrath is being revealed against **all** *ungodliness* (*asebeia*) and *wickedness* (*adikia*). *Ungodliness* points directly to wrong relationship with the creator. Morna Hooker describes the plight in graphic terms: 'man did not only exchange the worship of the true God for that of idols; he also exchanged intimate fellowship with God for an expression which was shadowy and remote, and he exchanged, too, his own reflection of the glory of God for the image of corruption.'[68] *Wickedness* points to wrong relationships within the created order – perverted and misused natural desires that lead to personal disintegration and social dysfunction. In their alienation, they suppressed the truth about

God. This probably includes the truth about the created order and its creaturely relationship to the creator in which the harmonious relations were intended to work according to nature. The term 'nature' can sometimes give the wrong impression, that is, that nature is somehow an independent object or entity which just 'is' and that we somehow operate outside of it and use it. But the more biblical perspective is 'creation', that is, the created order including humanity as created by and sustained by the love of the creator God.[69] Thus, the problem is the disharmony of all creation as a consequence of human disobedience; this is the reason for God's redeeming activity. 'The relation of these two terms [ἀσέβεια and ἀδικια] indicates that God's eschatological redemptive action for Israel is seen within the context of God's salvific act for all creation.'[70]

Ungodliness and wickedness presage the spiral into chaos. Paul describes the chaos in a series of statements and consequences that cumulatively make up the picture of the alienated state of the Gentile world. At root, the dysfunctional society in which the Gentiles live is a consequence of distorted relationships. Once the primal relationship with God is distorted, darkened minds, perverted desires and chaotic social relationships follow as night follows day. The chaos in the world is the open and running sore of human alienation from God. God has allowed humans to assert their independence from him and in doing so, suffer the consequences of their choices. They are acting against nature, the way things were intended to be by the Creator, with the inevitable result of chaos.[71]

If Adam lurks in the shadows in Romans 1, he now takes his place as one of the major protagonists in Romans 5. Israel's failure is also on view.[72] In Romans 5:12 Paul makes explicit what he had only hinted at in chapter one: *sin came into the world through one man.*[73] The language he uses is important. First, it is not that Adam, the sinner, introduces sin to the world but rather that Adam, the human, is the one through whom sin gained entry into the world. Again this makes it clear that sin is *not* the natural consequence of creatureliness. Adam introduces sin into the world, but all of humanity since Adam has entered into the human condition in a context in which sin is already 'in' the world. This corporate solidarity is essential to the notion of 'in Adam' just as it is essential to the notion of 'in Christ'.

Second, *death came through sin*? Paul is, of course, particularly interested in 'spiritual' death. Neither the primeval narratives nor Paul address the question of whether humans (would have) died before the fall (or indeed, animals, fruit flies, or vegetation!). Paul's main point is clear, however: *death spread to all*. Death as it is currently present and experienced in the world came through sin and the universality of sin is demonstrated by the universality of death. But once sin enters the world, death itself, inextricably linked to sin, becomes a power.

Third, the precise significance of the *crux interpretatum* at the end of Romans 5:12, the celebrated phrase, *eph' hō pantes hēmarton*, is as disputed as ever. At the very least, Paul is saying that people all sin and all die because they sin.[74] 'No one ... escapes the reign of death because no one escapes the power of sin.'[75] We must not, however, make Paul sound too individualistic. Paul is speaking primarily of people groups in both cases, not individuals. He uses universalistic language in Romans 5:12–21 to describe the effect of the free gift that *leads to justification and life for all* (5:18).[76] This, then, is about two groups – 'in Adam' and 'in Christ' – and not primarily about individuals within their groups. Hence, the usual focus on the fate of each *individual* caught in the nexus of sin and death tends to obscure Paul's main point.

Paul wishes to argue that the *corporate solidarity* that flows from the righteous obedience of the one righteous person, Jesus Christ, is more than a match for the *corporate solidarity* of disobedience that flows from Adam. The solidarity in Christ's obedience leads to abundance of grace, the free gift of righteousness exercised in dominion in life, and to justification and life for all. This is set against the solidarity of sin and death in Adam. This abundance of grace is necessary because, as Wright explains,

Christ did not begin where Adam began. He had to begin where Adam ended, that is, by taking on to himself not merely a clean slate, not merely even the single sin of Adam, but the whole entail of that sin, working its way out in the "many sins" of Adam's descendants and arriving at the judgment spoken of in 1:32; 2:1–16; and 3:19–20.[77]

Consequently, 'the interpreter should not reduce ... [these verses] only to a discussion of the implications of justification for the individual believer. By using biblical language for the restoration of God's people, they constantly situate the individual within the wider community.'[78]

If Paul thinks primarily of the solidarity in sin in Romans 5, in Romans 6 he thinks primarily of sin as a power affecting both people groups, Jew and Gentile alike. Paul's contrast between being 'in Adam' and 'in Christ' is now taken further in response to the outrageous suggestion that the superabundance of God's grace should encourage people to *continue in sin* (6:1). The notions of *solidarity* in the human condition and sin as a *power* are brought into juxtaposition with the notion of sin as the chaos-causing and peace-shattering *behaviour* that emerges within that solidarity and under that power. In Paul's view, then, sin is also a power.[79] It exercises its baleful authority over those who are in the solidarity of Adam. Its reign depends upon the allegiance of its servants. It might even be argued that sin's 'existence' as a power is essentially parasitic, that is, it feeds upon the manifestations of its own rule.

This metaphor of power is important. Paul contrasts 'the present age' held in the thraldom of 'sin' and 'death' and their unwilling servant, 'law', with 'the age to come', which has already been inaugurated in the life, death and resurrection of Christ. These two spheres of power locate all humanity either under the reign of sin and death or in the reign of God through participation in the obedience of Christ Jesus. Paul is at pains to emphasize the absurdity of living in two spheres at once, the sphere of 'sin' and the sphere of 'Christ'. The language Paul uses here is transfer language. Those who are in Christ have been transferred from the realm of sin's dominion to the realm of God. Of course, as Gaventa points out, 'To be freed from the power of Sin is not the same thing as being without flaw or incapable of transgression (sin in the lower-case). On the other hand, being free from the power of Sin means that the gospel actually does change human lives.'[80]

In Romans 7 Paul describes the effect sin has had on the law and the flesh. Sin has actually taken over the flesh and is directing people. As Ziesler comments, 'All are trapped and controlled by the power of sin whether they like it or not ... Sin is slavery, although it begins by consent.'[81] Paul puts it this way: *In fact, it is no longer I that do it, but sin that dwells in me* (Rom. 7:17).[82] What does Paul mean?

First, just as sin has perverted the law and used it for its own nefarious purposes, so sin has invaded, as it were, humanity and now 'dwells', like a squatter, within. Paul is, of course, careful to avoid any sense that Torah is the *cause* of sin. Rather, sin has used the Torah for its own ends. Sin, not Torah, has brought Israel to its current plight in which the law has proved to be powerless to redeem. The Torah, however, remains *spiritual; but I am of the flesh, sold into slavery under sin* (7:14). In the same way, 'flesh' *per se* is not the problem: it is sin. Nevertheless, this is a reminder that sin is not wholly external. This removes 'the devil made me do it' from the litany of human self-justification because, as Moo puts it, ' "I" am ultimately at fault; certainly not the law, not even sin. It is "me" and my "carnality," my helplessness under sin that enables sin to do what it does. "Sin" has invaded my existence and made me a divided person, willing to do what God wants but failing to do it.'[83] Paul's corporate language here is clearly personal as well, perhaps even autobiographical.[84]

Second, Paul is saying that the power of sin has subverted even the desire to obey God. People are powerless to save themselves because even their motivation has become tainted due to sin's invasion of human existence. The solution to this plight, therefore, must be more than the defeat of sin as a power. That would be dealing with the enemy without. Humankind exists as fallen flesh that is *subject to* and *invaded* by sin producing darkened minds. This is why Paul's solution to the condition is set out so succinctly and clearly in Romans 8:3 – *For God has done what the law, weakened by the flesh, could not do: by sending his own Son in the likeness of sinful flesh, and to deal with sin, he condemned sin in the flesh.* The key phrase here, *the likeness of sinful flesh,* means that Christ takes on our fallen humanity and redeems it. As Thomas Schreiner concludes, 'The Son did not merely resemble human flesh but participated fully in sinful flesh.'[85] This is not to be understood in any static, once-for-all-time sense, however. Nor does it make Jesus a sinner against God's law. Rather, he is born into our existence, lives in our fallen flesh, sanctifying it by his ongoing perfect obedience and in his death and resurrection defeats sin and death.[86] By taking on our human condition just as we are, he defeats sin through his obedient life and death and makes it possible, through the Spirit, that the inner dynamic of the law might be fulfilled in us.

So who is the 'wretched I' of Romans 7? Greathouse is typical of most recent commentators, taking the view that it refers to the experience of non-believers. 'If chapter 7 is autobiographical – relating the personal experience of Paul, it must be understood as a retrospective reassessment of his pre-Christian Jewish experience from his later Christian perspective.'[87] This is not, however, Paul's unique story. It is the story of those under the domination of the Law.[88] However, there are significant exegetical voices raised against this position.[89] In fact, says Moo, 'the interpretation of vv 14–25 in terms of "normal" Christian experience was typical of Lutheran and Reformed theology right into the twentieth century and is still widespread.'[90]

This view that Romans 7 describes the normal Christian life arises out of the eschatological tension in Pauline theology between the already and the not yet. Most scholars agree that the 'between the times' character of the present experience of the people of God runs like a thread in all of Paul's theology. The liturgical phrase, 'the world, the flesh and the devil' aptly summarize the context in which the holy life of God's people is to be lived. Paul frequently reminds his readers of the 'not yet' of our present experience. The body, Paul says, is mortal.[91] Paul expresses the tension particularly in Romans 8:10–11, 22–23. Christians live in *the mortal body*, which is subject to death and decay because of sin.[92] The mortal body will only be fully redeemed at the resurrection.

Furthermore, Christians suffer and are weak in solidarity with creation itself, living as they do in mortal flesh, fashioned from the dust of the earth and as part of creation. Because creation itself shares in the consequences of the human condition, Christians remain caught in the nexus of sin and death, part of their daily experience as believers. The ultimate redemption of creation awaits the ultimate redemption of the people of God.

Paul also thinks that cosmic opposition to God's rule has not yet ended, even if it has already, in principle, been defeated (see Col. 2:15 and Eph. 6:6). We live in a hostile environment in solidarity with people who remain alienated from God and a created order that is also subjected to futility. Therefore, as Stuhlmacher says, 'although the Christian is not "a sinner and righteous at the same time," the Christian is nonetheless "righteous and open to temptation at the same time," and will remain this way until he or she is taken by Christ into eternal glory (cf. Phil. 3:20f)).'[93]

These points are weighty. But this need not lead to the conclusion that Paul thinks the *normal* life of believers is one of tension – like rabbits caught in a headlight of a car. This picture of mortality, damage, and vulnerability must be balanced by the 'already' experience of the Christian.

First, even in this 'between the times' existence, Paul is quite clear that the Christian life is not to be characterized by a divided mind: *To set the mind on the flesh is death, but to set the mind on the Spirit is life and peace ... But you are not in the flesh; you are in the Spirit, since the Spirit of God dwells in you. Anyone who does not have the Spirit of Christ does not belong to him* (Rom. 8:6–9). Clearly, the 'mind set on the flesh' is an orientation of life[94] which contrasts with the mind set on God. Hence, while Christians remain in mortal/fallen flesh and retain creaturely solidarity in Adam, they are now part of the new solidarity in Christ and that solidarity is to determine their essential existence (8:10 – *If Christ is in you, then although the body is dead because of sin, yet the Spirit is life because of righteousness*). The holy life is lived daily in the Spirit in a very unpromising context. But with the mind set on the Spirit, believers no longer owe any allegiance to the old solidarity, the old way of being. The mind is set on the Spirit.[95]

Second, the whole life of believers is continuously offered to God in grateful response to the grace proffered in Christ (Rom. 12:1–2). In this context, the character is transformed by the renewal of the mind (see the contrast to the darkened mind of Rom. 1:21). Paul thinks of this as a process (see Phil. 3:12–15) that characterizes the life of God's holy people. Indeed, the paraenetic sections of the epistles are an essential part of Paul's theology. They set out the way God's holy people, comprised of Jews and Gentiles as the renewed covenant people of God, are to live out their mission of reflecting the love of God to the world within their own community.

Third, it is very difficult indeed to see how Romans 7:14 – *I am of the flesh, sold into slavery under sin* – can be a description of believers in light of the indicates in chapter 6 and, in particular, *But thanks to God that you, having once been slaves of sin ... you, having been sent free from sin, have become slaves of righteousness* (Rom. 6:17).[96]

One must take the tension between the already and the not yet with the utmost seriousness. But to describe Paul's view of the Christian life in terms of Romans 7 rather than Romans 8 is to tip the balance too far towards a pessimism which does not take full account of Paul's optimism of grace. The 'wretched I' of Romans 7 is not the normal Christian life, however often it seems to be the case in experience. That normal life is better described as peace with God.

5 Peace with God

Therefore, since we are justified by faith, we have[97] *peace with God through our Lord Jesus Christ*, writes Paul in Romans 5:1. Paul frequently uses the word 'peace'[98] to point to the character of God's gift to his people. In his view, the peace of God encompasses reconciliation with God and people, integration and wholeness of person and life. Peace is present when relationships between God and his people, between brothers and sisters, and with the created order in general are love-based and harmonious. Peace is the opposite of chaos, that is, anything that is contrary to God's order (see 1 Cor. 14:33).

When seen within two contexts, the societal and the personal, the peace of God becomes descriptive of the life of God's holy people. First, at the societal level, the peace of God stands in stark contrast to the Pax Romana, maintained by brutally crushing all revolt under the feet of Roman legions and a grotesque parody of the all-encompassing peace of God. Peace, genuine peace, is never achieved by military power, a lesson taught by history but never learnt, it seems. The people of God attach great importance to peace in societal terms because it is a fundamental manifestation of God's presence amongst his people. God's people are to be peacemakers – modelling peace themselves in their life together and being agents of it in our world. We shall return to this theme in a later lecture.

Second, peace at the societal level is predicated upon personal reconciliation with the holy God. Thus Paul can pray explicitly for his Thessalonian readers, *may the God of peace himself sanctify you entirely* (1 Thess. 5:23). This is a collective need – both Gentiles and Jews are alienated from God. The tragic stories of Adam and Israel can only be made right in Christ.[99] Christ is the magnetic pole, as it were, of all of God's purposes as expressed in Israel. All that God begins to do through Israel, despite its disobedience, he brings to fruition in Christ, the Israelite par excellence. In being the representation of Israel, Jesus attracts all the burden of alienation carried by humanity as a whole.[100] Christ's obedient death and resurrection sets in motion the final fulfilment of God's promises. Christ takes into himself the consequence of sin and is vindicated by God in resurrection, thereby removing the sting of death and robbing it of its victory. In a masterful summary of his gospel, Paul writes, *God sent his son, born of a woman, born under the law to redeem those under the law, so that we might be adopted as children of God* (Gal. 4:4–5).

God has acted in Jesus who, Paul says, was *put to death for our trespasses and raised for our justification.* We might have expected that Paul would say that Christ was put to death for our justification and raised for our sanctification. But for Paul, the death and resurrection are the same salvific act. We are put into a right relationship in and through Christ. 'If justification entails our transfer from a dominion of death to one of life, then the cross alone does not bring justification ... it is Christ's death and resurrection as a *total* event that procures justification.'[101]

The sanctification of people is the consequence of this. This is more than just a right relationship. It is also a transfer from one sphere of power to another as we have already seen. Because of Christ's death and resurrection, he tells his readers, *you also must consider yourselves dead to sin and alive to God in Christ Jesus* (Rom. 6:11). The defeat of death by the resurrection of Christ is the key sign that the transfer of allegiance to God's sphere of power is more than a legal fiction awaiting the final verdict. It is already a transfer. Reconciliation with God through participating in the obedience of Christ is the beginning of a different life. For Paul, the reconciliation is the first stage, the *justification*, but the life that is lived as God's new people and the hope for the future is based upon the resurrection. We have been brought into a right relationship and transferred to the sphere of God's power.

We must be clear here, however. Paul never sees the peace of God as a trouble-free life. In Paul's view suffering is the normal lot of the faithful community and is part of God's call to be his agents of reconciliation. We are called to live 'cruciform'[102] lives. Although suffering is not to be sought, it is to be embraced because it produces strong character leading to hope.[103] Paul believes that God has poured out his spirit on all who are believers (see Rom. 8:9b). This is not something that awaits the last days – for Paul the last days have already arrived. The coming of the eschatological spirit is confirmation that God has already acted. So he notes that *hope does not disappoint us because God's love has been poured into our hearts through the Holy Spirit that has been given to us* (Rom. 5:5).[104] And *nothing will be able to separate us from the love of God in Christ Jesus our Lord* (Rom. 8:29b).

In Romans 5 Paul initially points to the ultimate goal of God's good purposes: *we will be saved by his life* (5:10). But he also bases his whole Christian ethic on living in the power of the resurrection. It is in the resurrection of Christ that Paul believes that the dominion and power of death and sin are confirmed as broken: *just as sin exercised dominion in death, so grace might also exercise dominion through justification leading to eternal life through Jesus Christ our Lord* (Rom. 5:21).

The metaphor he uses to make this point centres on baptism and the death of Christ. According to Romans 6:1–11, Christians are united with Christ in his death. In fact, Paul uses the baptismal act in a metaphorical sense of dying and rising with Christ. But he is also careful to maintain the eschatological tension that informs his thinking throughout. We have died with Christ – our participation in Christ is a decisive death to the power of sin. This is a statement of fact – if we are in Christ, we have died with him in his once-for-all death.

In a very graphic expression, Paul states *ho palaios hēmōn anthrōpos sunestaurōthē*, translated by the NRSV as *our old self was crucified with him*. The meaning of this passage that is most consistent with Paul's ongoing discussion here has to do with the end to the old pattern of living, our old solidarity in Adam. William Greathouse translates this phrase as 'our career as sinners is over.'[105] So Paul says that our old mode of existence has ended in our identification with and participation in Christ's death. This must mean, then, the end of sin's reign. So, on the one hand, we are already dead to sin and walk in newness of life (Rom. 6:4). On the other hand, we still live in mortal flesh. Paul knows that though *the body is dead because of sin ... he who raised Christ from the dead will give life to your mortal bodies also through his Spirit that dwells in you* (Rom. 8:10–11). But Paul's emphasis here is the already: those in Christ are dead to sin and walk in newness of life.

That is why Paul then goes on in Romans 6 to give a number of imperatives. In simplest terms, his argument is this. Given the facts that you are dead to sin because you have been buried with Christ in a death like his, and that in his death the old way of being in Adam has been brought to an end for those in Christ, how shall you live? The answer comes in a number of exhortations Paul gives to his readers. Don't let sin exercise authority in your bodies. Stop presenting yourselves for wickedness. Stop being 'slaves' of sin.

Here Paul uses the familiar language of addiction to describe the condition of people apart from Christ. Once you are a slave to sin, you are on the downward spiral of sin leading only to death. Instead, be slaves of righteousness. In that way of living, the result is sanctification, the way of living and being in relationship to Christ. Right living leads to eternal life. There is no third way. In this new life, escape from sin is possible but not a foregone conclusion. Romans 6:18 is the crucial verse; righteousness is the power of God in Christ, under which believers live. Sanctification is the outworking in concrete terms of the new relationship we have in Christ; 'holiness/sanctification has moral connotations very often but behind these is the notion of belonging to God and being fit for him, sharing his holiness.'[106] As Greathouse notes, 'Since [holiness] exists only by virtue of a sustained relationship of loving obedience to the holy God, it can never be conceived of as a human possession.'[107] Thus Paul can urge his readers to be what they are in Christ through the Spirit because they have Peace with God.

Chapter Two

Holiness and the Holy Spirit

1 Life in the Spirit

In the last chapter, we saw how the good news of God's righteousness is displayed in active love by bringing his alienated creatures into a renewed relationship with himself. This is, in essence, the point of salvation. We also saw that Paul believes that putting right skewed relationships has been God's intention right from the disastrous disobedience of Adam. The call of Abraham and God's promise to him was always for that purpose. Then God creates and calls a people for himself, a people who would reflect his very character, would model his holiness before the rest of the created order and put into practice the relationship with creation that was intended for them from the beginning. While Abraham trusted in the faithfulness of God, the faithlessness of Israel was notorious. This left Paul with a hypothetical problem – does this mean that God himself would prove to be unfaithful? Such a conclusion is dismissed as preposterous. God could always be trusted – his promises never fall.

The good news is, according to Paul, that God honours his promises. He sends his son, born of a woman, born under the law for the sake of those under the law so that all of humanity could be adopted as children of God. In Paul's view, this is no afterthought; Paul is bold enough to argue that Christ is explicitly part of the OT story (1 Cor. 10:4, 9). Although this may surprise us, what is clear is that all the hopes and promises that are part of Israel's calling are gathered up in Christ, the perfectly obedient son of God, son of Adam, son of Abraham. In Christ the whole direction of God's good purposes comes to rest; Paul writes that *Christ is the telos of the law* (Romans 10:4). Believers, now in a new and right relationship with God in Christ, are enabled by the Spirit to live as God's holy people. This is a dynamic relationship to the holy God through participation in Christ. In this new sphere of God's power, people are transformed into who they are intended to be. This is clearly in continuity with the call to be a holy people from Paul's ancestral heritage. In the succinct statement of Gorman, 'As a Jew, Paul knows that to be holy is to be *God-like*; as a Jew in Christ, he know that to be holy is to be *Christ-like*.'[1] We concluded last chapter by summarizing Paul's imperatives to his readers in this way: *become what you are in Christ through the Spirit*. To put it another way, they are to be God's holy people through the Spirit.

Interestingly enough, however, up to this point very little has been said about the Spirit. Part of that is due to the way in which Paul writes Romans, the text that has been our primary source for the discussion up to this point. He does not write in a lineal fashion – this is not a systematic theology. Rather, he introduces a theme only to return to it again at a later point. This enables him to come at his overall theme from a variety of perspectives.

The connection between the Spirit and the holy life is a case in point. The Holy Spirit is central to Paul's whole argument in Romans even if he introduces the term rather late in the discussion. In fact, Paul flatly asserts: *Anyone who does not have the Spirit of Christ does not belong to him.* This simple statement is rather important for understanding Paul – there is no such person as a Christian in whom the Spirit does not dwell.

But Paul's first reference to the Spirit follows his sustained discussion of the revealed righteousness of God by which God acts to bring people into a right relationship with himself. For Paul, 'the immediate effect of God's grace is the outpouring of the Holy Spirit into the human heart.'[2] Hence, Paul makes a key assertion: *God's love has been poured out in our hearts through the*

Holy Spirit that has been given to us (Rom. 5:5). Most commentators[3] take the phrase *hē agapē tou theou* as a subjective genitive,
that is, 'God's love for us', rather than the objective genitive, 'our
love of God'. There are good reasons for this. Nothing in Paul's
epistles suggests that our love for God is a self-generated affec-
tion. It is always founded upon the grace of God. But Paul's
dense statement in this context may at least imply 'our love
for God'. The assurance believers have that God loves them is
through the witness of the Spirit poured out in their hearts. But it
also includes the idea that the Spirit places and releases God's
active and seeking love in our hearts. This is the work of the
Spirit in the life of believers – a point Paul repeatedly makes elsewhere by insisting that believers fulfil the law of Christ, the law
of love, through the power of the Spirit. In the words of N. T.
Wright, 'to find in one's heart a Spirit-given love for God is itself
more than consolation. To realize that this love fulfils the central
command of Torah is to discover oneself to be a member of the
renewed people of God.'[4]

Paul's language and understanding of holiness is thus
implicitly Trinitarian. Gorman puts it this way: 'Holiness is the
call and the will of God the Father; it occurs in Christ, who
defines holiness for the church; and it is effected by the Spirit,
who is the *Holy* Spirit.'[5] This Spirit is the 'holy' Spirit, not only
because this is the designation given to the third person in the
Trinity but because it is the Spirit who is active in producing
holiness.[6] As far as Paul is concerned, Gordon Fee observes,
'The Spirit is both the Spirit of Christ and the Spirit of God,
whom God has sent into the hearts of believers, thus pouring
his love into them, circumcising their hearts, sanctifying them.'[7]
The love between the creator God and his people, who has
poured out his love on his people, as well as the love in the relationships within the new people of God (see Rom. 8:15, 35, 37,
39; 13:8) underlies the remainder of the epistle. Thus holiness
and holy living are not, in Paul's view, optional extras in the
Christian life. They flow from the very love of God through the
Spirit, a love that includes all of his creation. As Nwachukwu
argues, 'Christian existence under grace implies that the new

life of the Spirit is given as a requirement placed on believers to lead creation to the praise of God's glory.'[8]

This is clearly Paul's thought in Romans 15:16 when he explains his mission, the intent of which is 'the making holy of the Gentiles.'[9] The obedience of faith 'is a phrase coined by Paul [by which] he gives voice to the intention of his missionary labours, viz., to make people of all nations faithful covenant-keepers by virtue of trust in Christ and union with him'.[10]

Paul's converts are the called ones of the holy God, *hoi hagioi*, 'the saints'. This is not just a tag for identification purposes, however. As Peter Oakes notes, Paul's designation of Christians as *hoi hagioi* 'represents a bipolar model of holiness rather than a progressive one: people are "holy" or "not holy" rather than holiness being a quality people have in varying amounts.'[11] Oakes shows convincingly that Paul's holiness language to describe Christians in Rome 'represents a sharply defined boundary [between Christians and non-Christians]: all Christians are holy, non-Christians are not ... Becoming one of "the holy people", in Paul's terms, is not a minor and unimportant matter.'[12] This, in fact, is a general characteristic of God's people throughout the Pauline epistles. But it does not make them a people who withdraw from society. Paul strenuously rejects that view. Rather, 'holiness for Paul means being different from but still located within the host environment.'[13] Therefore, 'their communities are not ordinary but holy.'[14]

This view is completely consistent with Paul's understanding of where the people of God now find themselves in God's grand scheme. They are people at the turn of the ages. The life, death and resurrection of Christ mark the boundary between the present age and the age to come: if Christ is raised, the new age has begun and it is the new age of the Spirit. And the new people of God, the Spirit people, are now being called into existence. Among the signs of the inauguration of the new age, according to Luke, has been the fact the outpouring of the Spirit on all flesh (see Acts 2:17); this is clearly reflected in the Pauline tradition in Titus 3:4–7. Paul never says anything directly about Acts 2, but he clearly reflects the same apostolic belief that the promise of God is being fulfilled.[15] In Romans 5:5, however, Paul's starting point seems to be Ezekiel 36:25–27, rather than Joel 2:28–32. This is an eschatological event, in which the people of God are already experiencing God's ultimate good purposes in the present.

This event is not merely external. Paul speaks of being in Christ and the Spirit living in people, so Paul believes that Christ, through the Spirit, indwells the people of God. And that is inextricably linked to the love of God in the heart. The motivational centre for the new people of God will not, therefore, be a spirit of slavery but that of beloved children – love-based and grace-enabled response rather than coercion.

But what are the implications of this indwelling Spirit for God's people; this life in the Spirit? Central to the discussion is the contrast between what they were and who they now are. His view of humanity, particularly 'body' and 'flesh', set up the contrast between people of the flesh and people of the Spirit. Later we will look at several facets of this contrast to help us understand how he conceives of the life of God's holy people. A clear understanding of Paul's contrasts requires some attention to these two aspects of Paul's anthropology: 'flesh' and 'body'.

2 Paul's View of Humanity

Clarification of Paul's theological anthropology has taken an important step forward in the recent major work on Pauline theology by Dunn.[16] The starting point is Dunn's central thesis is that 'Paul's theology is *relational*. That is to say, [Paul] was not concerned about God in himself or humankind in itself … His concern was rather with humankind in relation to God, with men and women in their relationships with each other, and subsequently with Christ as God's response to the human plight.'[17]

Paul's fundamental anthropology is relational because it is wholly dependent upon his relational theology. Paul assumes that humanity is created in the image of God and, as such, humans are created as beings-in-communion, reflecting the

Being-in-Communion of God.[18] In human terms, as Dunn notes, 'Paul's anthropology is not a form of individualism; persons are social beings, defined as persons by their relations.'[19] Nevertheless, when taken out of Paul's context and placed in the context of modernity, Paul's choice of terms to describe humans has given rise both to individualism and to a division of humanity into parts. Humans cannot be understood this way.

Our earlier discussion has shown that the human context apart from Christ is one in which the three basic relationships are all damaged. Because the primary human relationship with the creator God is marred, human relationships with each other and the created order are also damaged and distorted beyond human repair. If God is to display his righteousness, his covenant faithfulness, these marred relationships must all be addressed. To put it in even starker terms, salvation is never individual but it is always personal. 'His doctrine of salvation is of man and woman being restored to the image of God in the body of Christ.'[20] And this salvation is lived out, 'worked out' (Phil. 2:11), in the context of human existence and the created environment.

'Body' and 'Flesh' deserve particular attention in this context. Both of these terms have a spectrum of meaning in Paul. The first, 'body', is important not only because Paul uses it as one aspect of humankind but also because it is used in phrases like the 'body of Christ' [*sōma christou*]. Paul can use it simply to describe the physical body which is, however, 'only one end of the spectrum'.[21] According to Dunn, 'σῶμα is the embodiment of the person. In this sense σῶμα is a relational concept. It denotes the person embodied in a particular environment ... it is precisely "bodiness" (corporeality, corporateness) which enables individuals as bodies to interact with each other, to co-operate with one another. The body is the medium of that interaction and cooperation.'[22] In that sense, the body is 'the [personal] embodiment of the whole person'.[23]

Sometimes Paul uses 'body' simply as a cipher for the whole person as seen from the perspective of a being living in the real world of physicality and relationship. In a key passage, Romans

12:1, Paul's appeal to *present your bodies as a living holy sacrifice* is followed by ethical exhortations, reminding his readers again that 'ethics is not an addendum to salvation but an inherent part of what the Christ-event means.'[24] They are to present their bodies to God, not meaning primarily as isolated physical beings, but 'precisely as bodies, themselves in their corporeality, in the concrete relationships which constituted their every living'.[25]

It is important to note, however, that in Romans 12:1, the term 'sacrifice' is singular and that this is a 'holy' and 'living' sacrifice [*ta sōmata humōn thusian zōsan hagian*]. This is the only conclusion that Paul can draw from his sustained discussion of the faithfulness of God to his covenantal promises and renewing his holy people. The emphasis here is, therefore, that the people together are to be the holy people of God, now comprised of Jews and Gentiles, who offer 'true sacrificial worship' thus allowing the Gentiles to enter into the privileges of Israel (see Rom. 9:4).[26] 'In short, σῶμα gives Paul's theology an unavoidable social and ecological dimension.'[27] Perhaps that is why Paul can say in Romans 8:12 that those who are living in the Spirit are to put to death the deeds (NIV – 'misdeeds') of the body (*tas pracheis tou sōmatos thanatoute*). Here he equates the life lived *kata sarka* with the deeds of the body, a recognition of the fact that the body is subject to decay and resurrection.[28] The body, therefore, is important to holy living.

The second term key term for us is 'flesh' [*sarx*]. This is far more ambiguous in Paul giving rise to wide-ranging debate over many issues. Translators have particular difficulty in capturing Paul's meaning without over-interpreting the text. Hence, some translators simply opt to render the term consistently as 'flesh' rather than resorting to tendentious translations.[29]

Although most commentators on Paul would disagree for good reason, Paul does not hold an overall negative view of the flesh in principle.[30] The flesh is not intrinsically evil because God created it. Full weight must be given to Paul's Jewish background. 'Flesh', *sarx*, is used in the Septuagint to translate *basar*, often with a neutral sense of the physical stuff of animal existence, 'human embodiment'.[31] Thus 'flesh' is a term that refers to human existence in all its frailty and temporality. This is a thoroughly biblical phenomenological assessment rather than a moral judgement. 'The problem with flesh is not that it is sinful *per se* but that it is vulnerable to the enticements of sin – flesh, we might say, as "the desiring I" (7:7–12).'[32]

But Paul can, and usually does, treat flesh in a more negative sense. Dunn is particularly helpful here, noting that Paul 'recognized something of importance in the more negative Greek attitude to existence "in the flesh", which he also wanted to affirm'.[33] This distinction, he continues,

> made possible a positive affirmation of human createdness and creation and of the interdependence of humanity within its created environment. Subsequently, in the "Hellenization" of Christian thought the negative overtones of fleshliness became more and more attached to human bodiness, not least to the creative function of sexuality ... Concupiscence, sexual desire, came to be regarded by definition as wicked. Virginity was exalted above all other human conditions. Original sin was thought to be transmitted by human procreation. The results of such denigration of sexuality continue to distort Christian attitudes to gender till this day.[34]

In Paul's view, the facts of human existence show that the flesh has actually been infected by sin. Paul uses 'flesh' as shorthand in some cases, to indicate the life lived in the sphere of, and under the power and control of, sin. Nevertheless, as we saw in the last chapter, sin is the problem, not flesh. Human rebellion against God has let lose a power that is beyond their control. The end is death – the destruction of the host.

3 Walking According to the Spirit, Not According to the Flesh

People in Christ have been freed from walking in the path leading to death. The contrast that Paul draws between living in

the Spirit and living in the flesh is genuine. The new people of
God, he says, are *living, not in the flesh, but in the Spirit (ouk este en
sarki alla en pneumati* – Rom. 8:9.) This is not a war zone – those
who suggest that the battle of Romans 7 is a description of the
normal Christian life have missed Paul's point. This is not the
situation in which the people of God find themselves. Rather, in
Paul's view, *we are discharged from the law, dead to that which held
us captive, so that we are slaves not under the old written code but in
the new life of the Spirit* (Rom. 7:6). All this is through life in the
Spirit. Paul is adamant about the life of those in Christ: *For the
law of the Spirit of life in Christ Jesus has set you free from the law of
sin and of death* (Rom. 8:2).

The dynamic character of the holy life is conveyed by Paul's
contrast between walking according to the Spirit and according
to the flesh. When Paul refers to walking, clearly he is not
talking about a state, but a dynamic ongoing relationship lived
in the sphere of God's power.[35] This is not then just a change of
allegiance, a transfer to the new sphere of God's power, but
gives a sense of the ongoing life of believers in Christ. Here now
we see how the real goal of the Torah, in its life-directing function, is fulfilled through those who are in Christ.

What has happened to enable believers to walk according to
the Spirit and to be free from the tyranny of sin, death and the
law? Paul's answer is that God himself has undone the damage
unleashed by his own created beings on all of the created order
as well as his Torah: *by sending his own Son in the likeness of sinful
flesh, and to deal with sin, he condemned sin in the flesh, so that the
just requirement of the law might be fulfilled in us, who walk not
according to the flesh but according to the Spirit* (Rom. 8:3–4). But
this is far more than a legal transaction in which the obedience
required of the law is fulfilled in us through incorporation into
Christ and is therefore merely descriptive.[36] As Schreiner
observes, 'Those who confine obedience to forensic categories
in 8:4 seem to miss rather badly the scope of Paul's argument.'[37]

The full identification of Jesus with our fallen humanity is
the way in which God destroys the power of sin in the flesh.
As Messiah, Jesus represented the whole people – his death is

the death of the old way of being in Adam – for all those in Christ.[38] Jesus' perfect obedience (that is, without sin) even to death is the way in which the old way of being has been brought to an end. As a consequence of his obedience, the purposes of God which are life (*the just requirements of the law*) are fulfilled in us, that is, in our own humanity as we walk, not according to our old way of being, but according to the new way of living – new life in the Spirit.

This is not, of course, a case of self-reliance as if believers could now exercise personal self-discipline and thereby follow a path of holy living that added up to walking according to the Spirit. Paul never takes the view that once we have become believers, we work out our salvation in our own strength. Paul would have little time for a self-centred, self-help model of holiness.[39] Indeed, contemporary models of Christian holiness that tend to equate holiness and wholeness are not far removed from this self-centred view and encounter some serious problems.[40] On the contrary, the just requirements of the law, gathered up in Christ, and summarized in the law of love, are now to be fulfilled in those who *walk in the Spirit*. Christ's faithful obedience, even to death (Phil. 2:8), is the basis upon which the law is fulfilled in believers. Previously, the power of indwelling sin has prevented fulfilment of the Torah's purposes. But now the presence of the indwelling Spirit in the people of God empowers the fulfilment of the Torah. To put it another way, the resurrection life of Christians, who walk in newness of life, a new way of being (Rom. 6:4), is now described as walking in the Spirit, the life-giving Spirit.

But it is also important to note that Paul does expect believers to work out their salvation. This is precisely the point that Paul makes in Philippians 2:12. Paul writes, *Therefore, my beloved, just as you have always obeyed me ... work out your own salvation with fear and trembling.* Ross Wagner cites Morna Hooker's perceptive words, 'What [Christ] does *for* us has to be worked out *in* us.'[41] In Wagner's view, Paul sees believers' salvation worked out in the transformed community 'of God's "holy ones" [which] is the vanguard of the outworking of God's rectification of the cosmos'.[42] Clearly, God's initiative and enabling power stands behind this call, but 'God is working among the Philippians, not apart from but in and through their own volition and action.'[43]

It is significant, of course, that this 'therefore' follows and depends upon the model of Christ set out in most clearly in the Christ hymn of Philippians 2.[44] This hymn is profoundly important for our understanding of holy living. According to Gorman, it 'reveals not only the narrative identity and holiness of Christ the obedient son, but also the narrative identity and holiness of God, the Father. This is a *counter-intuitive, counter cultural* and *counter imperial* form of deity... [which] was "ultimately not a *violation* of deity but an *expression* of it".'[45] Wagner notes that Paul offers the life of Christ outlined in this kenotic hymn as the model for his own life, and, by extension, therefore, the model of living that is to characterize those who imitate him. Thus, Christ's own life and death determines the shape of the life of God's holy people. They embody 'who they already are, by God's grace, in Christ'.[46] This includes, as Wagner puts it, 'the disciplined rejection of these old patterns of thought ... as the necessary corollary to embodying the new pattern that is now their own by virtue of their union with Christ.'[47]

But the key point has to do with the model of walking that Paul provides. It is the model of Christ, the crucified and risen one who because he was God, emptied himself and became obedient unto death. 'Kenosis is the *sine qua non* of both divinity and humanity, as revealed in the incarnation and cross of Christ, the one, who was truly God and truly human.'[48] This is the same pattern that we find in Romans 6, where Paul, on the basis of the believers' baptism in Christ, requires that they actualize in life the meaning of their union with Christ by rejecting their old way of life.

As noted earlier, Paul thinks of the whole law as fulfilled in the command to love – but, once again, this is not a self-generated love.

The general mandate to fulfil the law by walking in love is, on Paul's reading, to be found in Scripture itself. Thus, at a high level of generality, Scripture both commands and prefigures a certain "ethic," a way of life dedicated to God's service. Those in Christ – whether Jews or Gentiles – who walk in the Spirit now fulfil what the law requires, a life animated by the love of God.[49]

This is the love poured out in our hearts by the Spirit. The point is that those who are in the sphere of God's power through the Spirit and who walk in the Spirit fulfil the command of God as part of God's loving purposes for the whole of his created order.[50] Before Christ, 'the commandment that was "unto life" brought death because of sin residing in the flesh (7:10); now the same commandment brings life because of the indwelling Spirit.'[51] This walk, both in Romans 8:4 and Galatians 5:25 and modelled for us in Philippians 2:1–12, is, as Fee observes, 'in *keeping with the Spirit*, which means by that very fact that it is no longer "in keeping with the flesh".... the emphasis lies not on the "source" of one's walking but on that which characterizes the two different ways of life.'[52] God's holy people walk according to the Spirit, not according to the flesh, because the Holy Spirit of God dwells in them.

4 The Mind Set on the Spirit, Not on the Flesh

The dynamic of walking is closely linked to the renewed mind. Paul sees this transforming presence of the Spirit as affecting the mind as well. Paul, of course, sees humanity as more than rationality or emotion. As Dunn observes, '... the human being was not just rational and not just a bundle of feelings, but both ... [Paul] refused to reduce the wholeness of persons to rationality, but sought to maintain a balance between the rational, the emotional and the volitional.'[53]

An orientation of mind towards the flesh leads to death – it is still controlled by sin. For Paul the clear consequence of the marred relationship with God is the darkened mind: *their senseless minds were darkened [eskotisthē hē asunetos autōn kardia]* (Rom. 1:21). Paul uses two metaphors, 'heart' in Romans 1 and 'mind' in Romans 12, to describe the way of being and thinking that determines the orientation of persons.

In Romans 12, the Spirit-renewed mind, the orientation of the mind towards the Spirit, leads to life and peace because it is able *to discern what is the will of God – what is good, acceptable and perfect* [*eis to dokimazein humas ti to thelēma tou theou, to agathos kai euareston kai teleion*]. At first glance, this is an astonishing statement. Indeed, Paul has just quoted Isaiah 40:13, *'For who has known the mind of the Lord?'* [*tis gar egnō noun kuriou?*], with the rhetorical answer expected as 'no one'![54] And although Paul is in awe at the depths of the mystery of God's good purposes, he has been telling his readers up to this point that indeed the whole purposes of God have come to rest in Jesus, the *telos nomou* (10:4).[55] In that sense, the answer is that the mind of God, the direction of God's good purposes in Torah, has been revealed in Christ. It is on this basis that he moves to the sweeping and inclusive 'now therefore' of Romans 12:1, in which he gathers up the whole story of Romans to this point. The renewed mind indeed is able to discern the good and acceptable and perfect will of God.

Clearly, Paul does not here or anywhere else argue that humanity can discern the will of God apart from the work of the Spirit. On the contrary – senseless minds are darkened (Rom. 1:28). But, as Munzinger has shown, 'in both 1 Cor. 1:16 and Rom. 12:2 Paul's argument is the same: it is possible to discern God's will [because of] the transformation of those involved... defined by the Christ-event and empowered by the Spirit.'[56] Munzinger concludes, 'the mind set on the Spirit (Rom. 8:5f) signifies the pneumatological and cognitive process of appropriating and internalizing the Christ-event into character and mind. A renewal of intentionality and valuation takes place, which makes it possible for the believer to *want* to do the will of God.'[57] Dunn puts it this way: this is 'not a new capacity to discern God's will by rational means, but the integration of rationality within the total transformation of the person, the recovery of the mind's proper function from its "disqualified" state ... which was the consequence of human presumption

(Rom. 1:28)'.[58] This is why Paul can say that the mind is renewed *so that you may discern* [*eis to dokimazein*][59] the will of God.[60]

The contrast between the mind set on the Spirit and the mind set on the flesh is stark. The chaos and its ultimate expression of disintegration in death in Romans 1 that comes from the darkened mind is contrasted to life as the ultimate expression of that shalom, that peace with God, which lies at the heart of the restored relationship. This is community chaos in contrast to communal shalom. To be sure, the orientation of the individual can never be abstracted from the nexus of relationships in which persons exists. Hence, Paul can urge his readers in Romans 12:2 to resist the pressure to be part of the mindset of the world in opposition to God: *Do not be conformed to this world, but be transformed by the renewing of your mind* [*tou nomou*]. Just as he used the singular in 12:1 for 'body' to remind his readers of the community character of their offering, so here he uses the singular for 'mind' to imply the oneness of mind that should characterize their new life together (see Philippians 2:2). 'This singular mind belongs to the community', writes Greathouse. 'A Christ-shaped community mind "made new" may be "created to be like God in true righteousness and holiness" (Eph. 4:24).'[61]

But his concern is also on the person, the level of the motivation that determines action and affects the corporate mind, as it were. Paul states that you (plural) are to be transformed [*metamorphousthe*]. The renewed mind discerns the will of God written on the heart.[62]

All this sounds like a very optimistic transformation of the mind. But what about the real world, the world in which the slavery to sin has wreaked havoc on the whole being? What about the scars of damaged relationships, the fear arising from abuse, the diminished intellectual capacity as a consequence of substance abuse, the abusive churches, or any of the myriad of other real-life contexts in which the holy people of God find themselves on a daily basis? Does Paul's theology have anything to say to us? Because of these scars, is the renewed mind only a hope for the future?

Actually, Paul lives in the real world. He suffers personal loss and tragedy. He suffers physical cruelty, knows the depths of depression even to the point of despairing for life itself (2 Cor. 1:8–9). And he lives in the Roman Empire with all its ambiguities. So Paul's theology is set in the context of the real world. This transformation is not renewal through a crisis experience, like the reformatting of a hard drive, in which everything is erased and instantly re-programmed. Moo thinks of it as 'a life-long process by which our way of thinking is more the way God wants us to think'.[63] But even that does not capture what Paul means. His view is that the orientation of the mind is changed – it is the mind set on God. Within that orientation, then, the mind is both transformed and being transformed. It 'demands a continual perfecting, even of the transformed mind' within the context of the holy people of God 'marked by mutual love and accountability'.[64]

The bases for Paul's realistic optimism are theological. First, Paul's realism about the present is set in the context of his unshakeable resurrection hope. Through the power of God, Christ has been raised bodily from the dead as the first fruits of God's ultimate redemption of all things. *If Christ is in you,* he says, *though the body is dead because of sin, the Spirit is life because of righteousness. If the Spirit of him who raised Jesus from the dead dwells in you, he who raised Christ from the dead will give life to your mortal bodies also through his Spirit that dwells in you* (Rom. 8:10–11). Human weakness and mortality, including all the scars and pain associated with it, will be swallowed up in the victory of the redemption of our bodies in resurrection. We will say more on this in chapter four.

Second, Paul believes God's big purposes will be accomplished and that, through the Spirit, his people are part of that outworking. His discussion in Romans is set in the context of the work of the Spirit, arguably the focus from 8:1–28. Those who walk by the Spirit with their minds set on the Spirit are children of God and are joint heirs with Christ. But they also share in his suffering for and with the creation itself, sharing also in weakness. In these circumstances 'the "weakness" of believers is addressed and sustained by the Spirit's intercession, so it is fair to conclude that [Paul] understands all prayer as arising from an inarticulate realm that expresses human vulnerability at its depth.'[65] And God understands because of the Spirit's intercession in the inarticulate groans of God's people in solidarity with and on behalf of creation.

That brings us to the beginning of 'the climactic celebration of the thesis concerning the hopeful suffering of the children of God'[66] in Romans 8:28: *We know that all things work together for good for those who love God, who are called according to his purpose.* This much cited and sometimes abused verse is fraught with textual, translation and interpretation challenges.[67] Part of the problem is Paul's. His syntax here is not particularly clear; translators have had to make decisions that affect interpretation significantly. Nevertheless, in light of what has been said so far in this section of Romans, the general point is clear enough. Even in the midst of suffering, in the lives of those in whom the Spirit has poured out the love of God (Rom. 5:5), we know this for certain: God's good purposes, the redemption of the lost and establishment of his new creation, will be accomplished.

Furthermore, those who walk according to the Spirit, and who respond to God's love through the Spirit, are people on God's mission. 'In the context of this letter', writes Jewett, 'the "good" to be accomplished by this cooperation includes the daily work and congregational formation ... as well as the risky mission to Spain that they will be asked to support. The thrust of the argument is encouraging: despite adversity and the ongoing weakness of the congregation, the Spirit labors along believers in such tasks.'[68]

Paul's third response is this – *nothing will be able to separate us from the love of God in Christ Jesus our Lord* (Rom. 8:38). In short, the renewed mind is not the recovery of lost mental power, or removal from the real world, but the single-minded direction of living as the new people of God, that full identification with and obedience to the purposes of God. As N. T. Wright remarks, 'with all the ambiguities and perplexities of Christian moral life, there is such a thing as knowing and doing God's will, and that we are commanded to pursue it, as Paul indicates in 1 Cor. 3:18–23, humbly but confidently.'[69]

Paul concludes the contrast between life according to the flesh and life according to the Spirit with a resounding statement of fact. *But you are not in the flesh; you are in the Spirit, since the Spirit of God dwells in you. Anyone who does not have the Spirit of Christ does not belong to him.* So, they now are Spirit-people, not flesh-people. They are people of God, no longer slaves to sin. They walk by the Spirit, not by the flesh. But Paul does not collapse the future hope into the present; neither does he diminish the reality of the new life in Christ. As Wright notes, 'If someone challenged him and said that sin and death were just as powerful to them as they had been before their coming to faith, he would reply that they had not yet considered the seriousness of their baptism.' Wright continues, 'if someone claimed that, now they had been baptized, evil had no attraction whatever for them, he would no doubt reply that they had not yet considered the seriousness of sin … [But for Paul] the Christian … stands already on resurrection ground.'[70]

5 The Witness of the Spirit

For John Wesley, the witness of the Spirit in giving the assurance that believers are children of God is crucial.[71] It is for Paul as well. Paul thinks that it brings the narrative of God's redeeming action to the climax. He writes, *All who are led by the Spirit of God are children of God.* With this sentence Paul begins his summation of the redemption and release found in Christ – adoption as children of God. Paul sees this as the *present* existence of the people of God – they are the new and renewed children of God. All who walk by the Spirit instead of the flesh, who have the mind set on the Spirit instead of the flesh and are led by the Spirit, these are the children of God.

Once again, a rich Old Testament background lies behind Paul's thought here. In the phrase 'led by the Spirit', some scholars see an allusion to the children of Israel in the wilderness where they are led by the pillar of cloud by day and of fire by night.[72] The allusion is even clearer in 1 Corinthians 10:1–4. Paul writes, *our ancestors were all under the cloud, and all passed through the sea, and all were baptized into Moses in the cloud and in the sea, and all ate the same spiritual food, and all drank the same spiritual drink. For they drank from the spiritual rock that followed them, and the rock was Christ.* Here Paul is quite prepared to assert that God in Christ is present with the children of Israel in the wilderness. Clearly, Paul would be aware that this perspective would be news to his fellow Jews. But this is the conclusion to which Paul is driven by his encounter with the risen Christ and his radically altered understanding of the trajectory of Israel's story in which he now sees that the triune God has always been active. Israel's story is not a disconnected prolegomenon to the real story – it is an essential part of it.

This dwelling of the holy God amongst his people by fire and cloud is now described as the dwelling of the Holy Spirit of God in his people. They live as God's holy people because they are led by the Spirit and have put to death the deeds of the body. These Spirit-led people press forward to their inheritance rather than retreat into slavery – Exodus imagery is also prominent here. Free from the tyranny of sin, death and the law, the Spirit-led people are no longer slaves but children. Robert Jewett, citing Robert A. Atkins, states that 'this provides a fictive kinship relationship offering the advantages of privileges of future inheritance and present status.'[73] Earlier, Paul had drawn a contrast between the enslavement of sin leading to death with enslavement to righteousness leading to life (Rom. 6:18). His slight hesitancy in applying the term 'slavery' to righteousness is now clear – slavery is not the appropriate metaphor for children. Children of God are not led in fear back into slavery. This is the reason that God is called *"Abba! Father!"* by the new people of God and it is the Spirit who leads and indwells who is *bearing witness with our spirit that we are children of God.*

The very prayer to God as *Abba! Father!* is itself important. 'Since the Spirit impels believers to utter their prayers directly to their Abba, this is a powerful, experimental confirmation of their status as children of God.'[74] The goal of the story is this. If we are *children, then [we are] heirs, heirs of God and joint heirs with Christ*. As Spirit-indwelt people who are children of God, we are fellow heirs of Jesus Messiah and share in his victory, act as agents of God's good purposes for the world and, indeed, share in Christ's suffering, his costly love for the world. Many commentators think of sharing in the glory as wholly future.[75] But Paul sees this as a present, albeit, anticipatory sharing in the glory of the risen and conquering son – which he elsewhere describes as being *transformed into the same image from one degree of glory to another; for this comes from the Lord, the Spirit* (2 Cor. 3:18),[76] as we see the glory of the Lord. But the end is also in view – the ultimate victory of God in Christ when all of God's big purposes come to their conclusion.

Paul then elaborates on the presence of the Spirit in the life of believers. As the conclusion to his lengthy discussion for the Roman Jewish and Gentile believers to live in harmony and mutual respect, he writes, *For the kingdom of God is not food and drink but righteousness and peace and joy in the Holy Spirit* (Rom. 14:17). These are not human virtues nor abstract qualities[77] but are characteristic of those who through the Spirit are God's holy people. Paul could be alluding to Romans 5:1–5[78] but as the immediate context makes clear, these are the community-enhancing fruit of the Spirit and are a witness to the Spirit's presence in their midst in contrast to disputes about issues of food and drink.[79] As well as the Spirit's community-shaping work in the midst of the holy people,

> the Spirit empowers us to abound in hope in the present, and intercedes for us in the midst of our present weaknesses ... The life described by the Torah is now lived by the power of the Spirit; accordingly, the Spirit represents a new 'law' – that of life, given by Christ Jesus. As such the Spirit is the source of love, joy and peace in the present, as one awaits the certain future.[80]

But Paul is also clear that life in the Spirit now has the character of first fruits, not finality. The Spirit's presence in the people of

God is the pledge, the guarantee of the future (see Eph. 1:14). It is life lived in the eschatological tension between the already and the not yet. Thus, the Spirit is present in the 'not yet' of Christian existence as well as the 'already'. He is with us in our frailty and weakness, and in our solidarity with the rest of creation. We share in the longing for the completion of God's purposes including *the redemption of our bodies.*

Finally, Paul writes, *Likewise the Spirit helps us in our weakness; for we do not know how to pray as we ought, but that very Spirit intercedes with sighs too deep for words. And God, who searches the heart, knows what is the mind of the Spirit, because the Spirit intercedes for the saints according to the will of God* (Rom. 8:26–27). This, too, is the witness of the Spirit. As Jewett puts it, 'The holiness of believers thus entails an ongoing intervention of the Spirit, maintaining their relationship as children of God through the inarticulate groans they utter as well as their "Abba" acclamation as describe in vv 15–16.'[81] Wright sounds a similar note concerning the Spirit: 'just as it is the Spirit's task to inaugurate genuine humanness in the Christian in the form of holiness (vv 12–14) and the *Abba*-prayer, so here it is the Spirit's task to enable genuine humanness, that stance of humbly trusting God.'[82]

6 Sanctified by the Spirit

On two occasions, Paul explicitly speaks of sanctification by the Spirit. The first in 2 Thessalonians 2:13 occurs in a context in which he is encouraging his readers to stand firm in the face of some false teaching by reminding them that they have been chosen by God *as the first fruits for salvation (aparchēn eis sōtērian)* which is *through sanctification by the Spirit (en hagiasmō pneumatos).* For our purposes, there are three implications. First, Paul is identifying his converts as those who are part of God's elect people, part of God's holy people. This continues a theme from 1 Thessalonians where these Gentile converts to Israel's God now participate in the promises and demands of God's holy people. Second, in light of the ethical expectations set out by Paul in 1 Thessalonians, Paul's use of the term *hagiasmos* here emphasizes that the life of the community is to reflect the holiness of God.[83] Third, Paul also establishes a theme to be repeated in his later epistles – that 'there is no genuine conversion that does not include the sanctifying work of the Spirit.'[84] The Spirit not only is active in the ongoing process of sanctification of the people of God, but in the initiation of this relationship with God.[85]

The second reference occurs in Romans 15:16. In this masterful summary of his ministry through which he is leading up to a request that the Roman Christians join in supporting his mission to Spain, Paul writes *I have written to you because of the grace given me by God to be a minister of Christ Jesus to the Gentiles in the priestly service of the gospel of God, so that the offering of the Gentiles may be acceptable, sanctified by the Holy Spirit*. This summary is full of important points, not least the strong cultic and liturgical language: *minister ... priestly service ... acceptable offering*, all of which influence our understanding of *sanctified by the Holy Spirit*. In some ways, this is particularly remarkable, demonstrating the transforming character of the gospel. The Gentiles, who were at one time excluded from the holy, are now an acceptable offering (see Rom 1:9; 12:1–2).[86] Cultic language, however, should not obscure the clear ethical overtones of this passage, as Paul has already made abundantly clear in Romans 6 and will confirm in the next sentence when he speaks notes that his mission is to *win obedience from the Gentiles*.[87]

But for purposes, it is the last phrase, *made holy by/in the Holy Spirit* (*hēgiasmenē en pneumatic hagiō*) that is crucial. This phrase is 'emphasised by its position at the end of a complex statement'.[88] The cultic context requires that we understand being made holy first in terms of purity. Jewett comments, 'the set-apartness and purity of God's chosen people, separated from the degenerate Gentile world, comprising an island of vitality and decency, are now extended to the Gentiles ... the gospel extends holiness to the Gentile congregations.'[89] Second, both Jewett and Greathouse remind us that 'ethical sanctification should not be confused with individualistic notions of sanctification as merely a private "striving toward high ethical ideals."[90] Paul's concern is with the holiness of the Gentile churches as communities, with the transformation of their social life that comes from the empowering and hallowing presence of the Holy Spirit among them (as Rom. 12:1 – 15:13 shows).[91]

Although the precise phrase, 'sanctification by the Holy Spirit', is not used often by Paul (see also 1 Cor. 6:11), it is significant. It reminds us that the people of God are made and being made holy, that the Spirit is creating a people that is inclusive of all who are transformed by the Spirit, and that the work of God has a Trinitarian shape. It is also linked to the fruit of the Spirit and the gifts of the Spirit, to which we now turn.

7 The Fruit of the Spirit

The presence of the Spirit creating the holy people of God produces behaviour that issues from the Spirit. In Galatians 5:22–23, Paul identifies this behaviour as the fruit of the Spirit. In fact, descriptions of the holy life have often started from the fruit of the Spirit, complete with an analysis of each item on this list. But this kind of analysis does not really capture Paul's point here. This is not a list of human virtues that can be cultivated, watered and fertilized as if each virtue grew on a tree. Their origin is from God and their growth and development occurs only through the indwelling presence and guidance of the Spirit.

The context of Paul's description of the fruit of the Spirit is a warning against abusing the freedom Christians experience from the tyranny of law. If holy people do not live by the letter of the Torah, then how are they to live? Is there not a serious risk that people would simply return to their old ways in pagan culture? This is by no means an idle concern – Paul often addresses behavioural issues in the lives of his converts that are the legacy of their past. Paul warns against returning to the old way of being as a return to slavery both in Galatians and

Romans. In 1 Corinthians 6:9–10, Paul reminds his readers of their past so that they might not be tempted to return to it. He is aware of this danger, so while he affirms their freedom in Christ from the obligations of full Torah observance, he warns them not to use their *freedom as a means of self-indulgence* (Gal. 5:13). In fact, nothing would be further from the intention of Torah which is summed up in the single command: 'Love your neighbour as yourself.'

But how could they live that life of love? Answer: carry on living by the Spirit (Gal. 5:16). When they began their lives as the people of God, Paul notes that they started with the Spirit (Gal. 3:2). But life in the Spirit must be based on more than just a sacred memory – it must be an ongoing, life-shaping relationship, walking by the Spirit with lives controlled by and cooperating with the Spirit. God works with his people through his Spirit, 'not apart from, but in and through their own volition and action'.[92] It's a journey in which the orientation of the whole being is towards God and his purposes.

This orientation rules out community-damaging self-indulgence. Selfishness of any sort would be a complete denial of the presence of the Spirit in the community of faith. It could also point to a complete misunderstanding of the evidence of the Spirit's presence in the community. As far as Paul is concerned, evidence of the Spirit in the community of faith is, says James Dunn, 'not just as experience of surging emotions (Rom. 5:5; 1 Thess. 1:6), or of charismatic empowering (as in Gal. 3:5), or of inspired utterance (as in 1 Cor. 14) or of ecstatic experience (cf. Acts 2:4, 1 Cor. 12:2; 14:12)'.[93] All of these could be a form of self-indulgence. But, as Dunn continues, the evidence is rather 'experience patterned on Christ's (cf. Galatians 4:19) and as conforming to Christ's sonship (Galatians 4:6–7). It is precisely as the Spirit of the Son (Galatians 4:6) that Paul expected the Spirit to be known and acknowledged within the churches.'[94]

This life lived by the Spirit, who is the Spirit of the Son, naturally issues in the fruit of the Spirit that is entirely consistent with the cruciform character of Jesus' life. The Spirit enables the keeping of the commandments – summed up in the command to love neighbour as oneself. In this summing up of the Torah, Paul is at one with Jesus' own teaching on Torah. The summation takes Torah back to its roots and is both an intensification by getting to the heart of Torah as well as a freeing from any perfunctory obedience of the secondary interpretations of Torah. Thus the Torah has continuing moral force for those who are in the new age of the Spirit. In that sense, Paul understands clearly that

> in the gift of the Spirit these earliest Christians had experience the hoped-for circumcision of the heart of Deuteronomy, had experienced the hoped-for new covenant of Jeremiah, had experienced the hoped-for new heart and new spirit of Ezekiel. What must be noted, however, is that this hope did not refer to another law or another Torah ... The coming of Christ and of faith in Christ has brought emancipation from the law in its temporary, constrictive function (Gal. 3:19 – 4:7), of course. But nothing that Paul says indications that Christ has brought emancipation from the law as God's rule of right and wrong, as God's guidelines for conduct.[95]

The fruit of the Spirit is not about private well-being. None of these items is referring to a manifestation of the Spirit that is focused on the individual. Rather each item on the list is best understood in the context of social relationship. The fruit of the Spirit, the life of the Spirit in the community, flourishes in grace-restored relationships. So the Spirit-controlled and directed life is none other than the life of God's love lived out in relationships within the community. That is where the fruit of the Spirit is manifest; none of these virtues really is describing an inner tranquillity that exists apart from the well-being of the community. If we are created as social beings in the image of the triune God, then our redeemed existence is to model the love that is the very essence of the relationship between Father, Son and Spirit.

The opposite of life guided by the Spirit is life controlled by the flesh. When Paul contrasts the fruit of the Spirit with the works of the flesh, he is talking about two orientations of life. The works of the flesh are a depressing catalogue of community-damaging behaviour. But a life orientated to the flesh is not simply one that gives unfettered reign to self-indulgence in every sort of 'sin of the flesh'. Paul's thought is at once far more comprehensive and subtle, speaking primarily of distorted relationships emerging from the self-centred mindset. In the life of the flesh, the actions are controlled by self-interest, a life turned in on itself. 'Wrongness towards God, wrong use of the physical body, but especially wrongness in our dealings with one another are the things that betray our living "according to the flesh".'[96]

It should not surprise us that these categories of wrongdoing are very similar to those outlined in the Holiness Code in Leviticus 19 – 26. God has always called his people to live holy lives in community. Unholy living is not the way of the Spirit. The life of the flesh is human-based, self-centred and self-indulgent; the life in the Spirit is God-given, God-centred and issues in service to others. These orientations cannot co-exist. For those in Christ, the fleshly orientation of life is over. In language that will later be paraphrased in Romans 6:6, Paul writes, *those who belong to Christ Jesus have crucified the flesh with its passions and desires* (Gal. 5:24). This also means 'the birth of new desires and practices that "flesh out" the root meaning of cruciform holiness as self-giving, other-serving love of neighbor'.[97]

8 The Gifts of the Spirit

The final point to be addressed in this chapter concerns the gifts of the Spirit. A great deal of rather unhelpful and clearly unbiblical material has been spoken and published in recent years on this controversial topic. I have neither the time nor the inclination nor even, perhaps, the ability to engage directly with this material. Instead, I wish to highlight a few principles about Paul's understanding of the gifts of the Spirit in God's holy people.

Paul speaks of *charismata* in several places in his epistles. But he gives particular attention to them in Corinth because, as exercised by the Corinthians, some had become a problem in their worship. In the next chapter we shall consider some of Paul's concern about the celebration of the Lord's Supper in Corinth. But Paul is just as concerned about this aspect of their community worship as he is the celebration of the Lord's Supper. As far as Paul is concerned, worship is one context in which the life of the community in fellowship with the triune God is expressed. This, then, is more than a pragmatic issue of decorum in church order.

Paul doesn't deny that the Corinthians have been given gifts of the Spirit (1 Cor. 1:7). This may seem obvious, but needs to be stated lest it be suggested that Paul questions the legitimacy or genuineness of their gifts. Nor does he suggest that abuse negates their importance. Gifts are essential. Paul simply cannot conceive of the body of Christ without them.

In Corinth, however, the exercise of these gifts – in particular the more public and seemingly 'supernatural' gifts – seems to have been subtlety captured by the surrounding culture. The problems Paul encounters at Corinth suggest that their cultural context remains highly influential in their lives – that the Corinthians have not fully grasped just how counter-cultural the Christian community really should be.[98] Their problem seems to be an individualistic, even competitive, understanding of church life. So Paul 'struggles to alter the Corinthians' tendencies to individualism and boasting and tries to integrate the believers more fully into community and a sense of belonging to and serving one another in Christ'.[99]

In such a context, it should be no surprise that the most problematic gifts involve speech – prophecy and tongues – since oratory and public performance are prized in Corinth. The context of public performance and boasting has hijacked these gifts for personal self-satisfaction and an enhanced sense of spirituality. Paul addresses this by reminding the Corinthians about the purpose of these gifts. They are to be set in the context of the mission and purposes of God for his people. As Gorman perceptively observes, 'Paul's primary goal is to turn a *charismatic* community into a *cruciform* community and therefore a *holy* community, one in which all believers are in proper relationship to one another and to God the Father, Christ the Lord, and the Holy Spirit.'[100] Those whose gifts appear mundane or ordinary are every bit a part of the community as those who have been given more public gifts. And their gifts are as important to the community. Only in this way can the Corinthians model the holy community of God as well as being a witness of God's presence to outsiders.

Paul mentions nine gifts of the Spirit in 1 Corinthians. He also lists other gifts in Romans 12:4–8 and Ephesians 4:11. As Paul Njiru argues, Paul's 'intention is not to offer a systematic, exhaustive list of the χαρίσματα. Rather, he offers a representative list so as to affirm that other gifts of the Spirit – not only the gifts of inspired speech such as prophecy and tongues – are equally important for the edification of the Church.'[101] Thus, to restrict the number of gifts of the Spirit to those given by Paul in one or more of these passages is to misread completely his understanding of the community of faith, the significance of the presence of the Spirit in its midst, and the place of the holy people in God's bigger purposes.

The community of faith is the creation of God through the Spirit. It is bound together in the unity of the Spirit. The Spirit dwells in the community as a corporate body and within individuals who derive their very existence as God's people from the one body of Christ. The Spirit, then, gives to the body of Christ everything that is necessary for its life and mission. In Paul's view the inexhaustible resources of God are the source of the gifts poured out upon the church. When that is taken into consideration, it is clear that the spiritual gifts could never be confined to a set number. The gifts are many and varied. As Paul says later in Romans 12:5–6, *so we, who are many, are one body in Christ, and individually we are members one of another. We have gifts that differ according to the grace given to us.* The range of gifts God gives is infinite. He gives whatever gifts of the Spirit are needed in whatever circumstance.

Earlier, in 1 Corinthians 12:4–7, Paul sets the gifts of the Spirit in the context of God's essential being as the source of all gifts. Paul writes, *Now there are varieties of gifts, but the same Spirit; and there are varieties of services, but the same Lord; and there are varieties of activities, but it is the same God who activates all of them in everyone. To each is given the manifestation of the Spirit for the common good.* Several points of importance flow from this statement. First, Paul holds that the source of all of the manifestations of the Spirit is found in the triune God of grace. The implicit but unmistakable Trinitarian language, Spirit – Lord – God, is paralleled to the 'gifts – services – activities' sequence. The infinite variety of resources of the grace all has the same source. Everything that contributes to the health of the body of Christ is understood to have its origin in God.

The point is crucial. Instead of a distinction between 'supernatural gifts' from the Spirit that come from outside the individual, as it were, and 'natural' gift that are the possession of the individual and enhanced by the Spirit, Paul sees all gifts on a continuum of God's grace gifts. A hierarchical view of gifts would imply a hierarchical view of Father-Son-Spirit. Semantically, as Njiru argues, 'the term χαρίσματα in the Pauline corpus is ... applicable to a great variety of concrete manifestations of God's grace.'[102] Some may appear to be more obviously of a 'supernatural' origin – the gift of glossolalia gives that impression in 1 Corinthians; others, like hospitality or administration in Romans 12:6–8 appear to be enhanced natural gifts. But for Paul this is a false dichotomy. All gifts of the Spirit are under the control of the person who is exercising the gift (1 Cor. 14:32), eliminating this distinction between external and internal. The conclusion Munzinger draws about the gift of discernment would apply more generally, mutatis mutandis, to the whole question of the gifts of the Spirit; 'it is the difficult path in searching for a symbiosis of Spirit and mind that should be followed.'[103] Indeed, each of these gifts can be exercised in a way that is detrimental to the well-being of the community of faith and therefore no longer serves the community as God has intended.

Second, the distinction Paul draws is between the more public and more private parts of the body (1 Cor. 12:22–24), implying a contrast between the more spectacular and the more apparently mundane gifts. Hence, every gift that is exercised in the community of faith and in the mission of God's holy church is rooted in the unity of the Spirit and the love of God poured out into the hearts of the believers and upon the community as a spiritual gift.

From this it follows that these are gifts of the Spirit for the body to be used for the upbuilding of the body, not personal gifts for one's exclusive well-being. Whatever personal benefit Paul might have experienced from the gifts given to him (see 1 Cor. 14:18) – and he never tells us – his life is always lived for others.

It also reminds us that the gifts given by the Spirit can never be used as a badge of superior spirituality or evidence of advanced standing in the community of faith. For Paul, there is 'no qualitative distinction between gifts'.[104] If gifts are dividing the body, they are being used contrary to the purposes of God. In that circumstance, the gifts are neither an acknowledgement of the Lordship of Jesus nor of Christ's body.

All of this has to do with a fundamental issue about the health of the body of Christ. So Paul turns to body language in an attempt to re-shape their thinking and practice. The beneficial exercise of the gifts of the Spirit is best illustrated, Paul thinks, by the healthy body. These gifts are given to equip the body and enable it to function properly. Paul puts it this way in 1 Corinthians 12:14–25: *Indeed, the body does not consist of one member but of many .... as it is, God arranged the members in the body, each one of them, as he chose ... that there may be no dissension within the body, but the members may have the same care for one another.* There is no hierarchy of gifts that God gives. Rather, the key outcome in the variety of gifts functioning well in the body is that they enable mutual care, one for the other. Ephesians 4:15–16 captures Paul's underlying theology of the gifts of the Spirit: *we must grow up in every way into him who is the head, into Christ, from whom the whole body, joined and knit together by every ligament with which it is equipped, as each part is working properly, promotes the body's growth in building itself up in love.*

Love, of course, is what keeps the gifts of the Spirit in their proper perspective as means rather than ends in themselves.

That is why Paul says that without love, the gifts are simply sound and fury, signifying nothing (Shakespeare, *Macbeth*, perhaps alluding to 1 Cor. 13:1–2).

God's holy people are people of the Spirit. They are called by the Spirit, made holy by the Holy Spirit, walk by the Spirit, have the mind of the Spirit, are indwelt by the Spirit, receive the gifts of the Spirit, are empowered by the Spirit, pray in the Spirit, worship in the Spirit and bear the fruit of the Spirit. All of this language has its primary locus in the holy community of God – God's called holy people who are bound together by the Spirit. In our next chapter we look a little more closely at holiness and community in the context of God's Holy People.

Chapter Three

Holiness and Community in Corinth

1 Status, Sex and Temple

The community orientation of Christian holiness is a theme that has gradually been emerging. In our last chapter as we considered life in the Spirit we saw that the Spirit indwells the people of God and leads them. The Old Testament roots of that notion clearly has a community orientation – the pillar of cloud by day and the pillar of fire by night, God's presence with his people, is not a private experience of individual Israelites. Rather, the community is being led through the wilderness by God. We also saw that the orientation of the fruit of the Spirit, with its headline of love, is precisely the kind of outworking of love in the people of God that enables people to serve each other in community. These are not private virtues – indeed, none of them could be cultivated in isolation from community. Finally, in our brief look at the gifts of the Spirit, it became clear that these, too, are gifts given by God to the community for its well-being and its participation in God's mission.

Conversely, we also noted that the orientation to the flesh, seen especially in Paul's list of the 'works of the flesh', leads to chaos and disintegration of community. These are desires turned in on themselves and so become a form of perverted self-love. The end, of course, of this distorted love and abuse of God-given desires, is self-loathing and personal and community destruction – in Paul's language death or exclusion from God's kingdom.

This community orientation is central to Paul's thinking – and requires a re-orientation of the mindset of his converts to Christ. Perhaps that is seen most clearly in his Corinthian correspondence to which we now turn. As is well known, these letters are part of an ongoing dialogue – some might say dispute – between Paul and his converts. They can only be understood properly within the context of the cultural and societal norms of Graeco-Roman society and against the social history of Corinth around the time of Paul.

Although some scholars take the view that the new Christian movement took root essentially amongst low-status people – slaves, poor freedmen and the like, recent studies suggest a greater cultural diversity in the mix in Corinth.[1] Paul writes, in 1 Corinthians 1:26–28 [REB]: *My friends, think what sort of people you are, whom God has called. Few of you are wise by any human standard, few powerful or of noble birth.* Paul implies that there are some who were powerful, wealthy and of noble birth, but this is a minority in the community of faith. These people may well have been those who provided meeting places in their homes, perhaps leadership due to their education, influence and skills. They would also have had some disposable income [1 Cor. 16:2; 2 Cor. 8—9] – Paul does contrast the poverty of the Macedonian churches with the implied comparative wealth of the Corinthian churches. But there would also have been a very significant number of poor people in the community of faith as well, including domestic slaves (1 Cor. 7:21–23) and others without resources. 'The Corinthian church mirrors the steep social pyramid of culture', says Paul Sampley, 'in which there was no middle class'.[2]

In this honour–shame society, status and its accoutrements are particularly important. People aspire to high status. Some inherit it but others acquire it. And when they have it, they want others to know. It is not impossible that status-seeking could have influenced the exercise of spiritual gifts within the community, for example. Even more likely is that the 'I'm of Paul', 'I'm of Apollos', 'I'm of Cephas', 'I'm of Christ' game has overtones of social status enhancement. Ben Witherington III notes that these aspirants are often the most blatant in their display of their wealth: 'members of the *nouveau riche* were those most likely to affect culture by entertaining Sophists, preferring their more popular rhetoric of display and entertainment to serious discourse.'[3] This prominent display of wealth fits what Witherington calls the 'self-made-person-escapes-humble-origins' syndrome.[4]

Reference is frequently made to the immorality of Corinth, arguing that its infamy was so well known that the very name of Corinth became associated with immorality. As Winter notes, 'all seem to be aware that [the verb] "to Corinthianize" had, for centuries, referred to having sexual intercourse with a prostitute.'[5] But, as Winter himself notes, this has to be treated with some caution. Certainly a level of immorality commensurate with its character as an urban, diverse centre exists in Corinth. But Winter shows the references to Corinth's serious degeneracy date to earlier Athenian slander. In fact, Winter writes, the whole story of a temple to Aphrodite with a thousand cultic prostitutes in residence

> was a myth from the Greek period as there was no temple prostitution in the Corinth of Paul's day for two reasons—(i) The newly built first-century temple to Aphrodite was a small construction on the edge of the Acrocorinth overlooking this proud Roman colony; (ii) by this period Aphrodite, the patron of the new colony founded by Rome in A.D. 44 had been Romanized and was now known as Venus, the divine 'mother' of the imperial family. No longer the naked sex icon of the Greek period, she was now a well-clad and highly respectable goddess.[6]

Sexual issues are, nevertheless, prominent in 1 Corinthians as they are in the other epistles. For instance, In 1 Thessalonians 4:3, Paul's first ethical implication of being God's holy people is that they *abstain from sexual immorality* in order to be a holy community. It may even be part of the issue being addressed in the *Haustaflen* in addressing the treatment of slaves. A recent study has argued that Colossians 3:8 – 4:1, when read against the background of the conventional rights of slave holders over the bodies of their slaves, on the one hand, and Paul's concern for sexual propriety, on the other, points to the avoidance of using slaves for sexual purposes.[7] As Gorman notes, as far as Paul is concerned, 'sexual immorality (Greek *porneia* – "unlawful sexual intercourse ... including homosexual practice and sexual immorality in general"[8]) and cruciform love cannot co-exist, for *porneia* is a form of self-love, of self-indulgence that harms others and diminishes the holiness of both the individual and the community.'[9] It is also, as Johnson points out, 'tantamount to rejecting the gift of the eschatological Spirit whose purpose is to sanctify them, i.e., to enable their life together to publicly display *this Lord's* character/holiness before the eyes of the nations'.[10]

But in Corinth the problems go deeper than just sexual impropriety, however important that problem is. To focus upon the sexual issues without noting the wider cultural context, Winter observes, 'misreads the secular mores of Roman Corinth and obscures the important teaching on the breadth of Christian corporate and personal holiness that encompasses matters well beyond the sphere of their sexuality'.[11] The aberrant sexual behaviour (and the question of eating food offered to idols that he addresses later) are merely sub-sets of the deeper counter-cultural issues at stake for the new community of faith. This issue, for Paul, is essentially the purity of the holy people of God.[12]

A second point for our purpose is the importance of temples in Corinthian culture.[13] Various religious practices dominate all aspects of life from civic and public office to private rites of passage like birth and death. Temples and shrines command public space. Many highly visible ceremonies take place. Indeed, probably an 'overwhelming number of all public events were explicitly religious in character'.[14] Meals, for instance, have religious connotations because the general populace believe that the gods are active and devotion to them works. So many social meals are held in honour of a god who is thought to be presiding and present. Meals are joyous social occasions.

It is clear, then, that temples are crucial. Hurtado reminds us that 'people frequented them for a range of purposes and combined social and religious life and activities easily within their precincts.'[15] Temples are sacred sites but no one except the Jews thinks of them in terms of holiness. A god who calls his people to be a holy people living lives that reflect his holiness is not on the radar screen of the typical sophisticated Corinthian status-seeker. Ethical holiness is rarely an issue in Graeco-Roman religion – the gods themselves are just not interested in ethical purity.[16]

Here, of course, is a particular place of tension for the Corinthian Christians. How should they relate to the social structures of Corinthian society? On the one hand, should they cut themselves off entirely so as to avoid contact? Paul gives short shrift to that idea (see 1 Cor. 5:9–13). Or do they simply participate? There are dangers. For instance, 'One should not underestimate the place of sexual expression ... especially in connection with the dinner parties (*convivia*) that were often held in the precincts of pagan temples.'[17] And what about offerings in the temples? The imperial cult is honoured in a temple near the forum – does the Corinthian Christian who is part of civic government participate in the offerings for the emperor? Numerous shrines to other gods are also in Corinth including Apollo (god of prophecy), Aphrodite (goddess of love), Asclepios (god of health), Isis and Sarapis.

The idea of a temple being the abode of a particular god is common. Indeed, for Jews everywhere, the Temple continues to symbolize the dwelling place of God with the Holy of Holies being the very locus of God's dwelling amongst his people. Although there appears to be a wide variety of views about the sanctity of the actual Temple in the Second Temple period,[18] the notion of the temple as the dwelling of God helps to explain the importance of this particular description of the people of God in 1 Corinthians. The purity of the temple of God as the dwelling place for the holy God lies behind much of what Paul writes in 1 Corinthians.

2 The Temple of the Holy Spirit

The appropriateness of the temple metaphor for the Corinthians is obvious in cultural as well as theological terms. Paul starts with the notion that a temple is the divine dwelling place. But Paul's view of where God dwells has been radically altered. God has acted in Christ and Jesus' cryptic remark about 'a temple not made with hands' is now making sense. As we have already seen, Paul understands Jesus to be the locus of God's action. All of God's good purposes come to rest in Jesus and in him the fullness of God dwells bodily (see Col. 1:19). He also takes seriously the fact that God's Spirit has been poured into the hearts of all who believe (see Rom. 5:5; 8:9). Behind all this is the notion of the covenant people of God. Paul is clearly persuaded that these are the days when a new covenant, founded upon and enacted in Christ, has been established with the people of God, a point he makes very clearly in 2 Corinthians 3 and 4. Jews who accept Jesus as God's promised messiah and Gentiles who are now being gathered into the people of God, through Christ, the Jewish messiah, are the new covenant people. That new covenant is the one promised in Jeremiah 31:31–34 and Ezekiel 36:26–27.

But Paul goes further. Not only is Christ the dwelling place of the Holy God who, in turn, is the Holy One in the midst of his people,[19] the very image of God (2 Cor. 4:4), the people of God dwell in Christ as well. Paul's 'in Christ' language is one of his most characteristic phrases – language which resonates clearly with the mutual indwelling language of John. It points to the mutuality of Christ in his people and his people in him (see Jn. 17:20–23). This is why Paul moves so easily to the appropriation of temple language to describe the people of God. If Christ is the locus of all God's big purposes, and the direction and destination of the Torah, and if God has established a new covenant with his people that is made effective by participating in the life of the covenant-maker, the only conclusion to be drawn is this: the people of God are now the dwelling place of God. And the implications are profound. There is no need for a physical temple in which God can dwell because God through his Spirit has created a new people and indwells them. So Paul draws upon the Jewish temple metaphor filled with the significance of the dwelling of the holy God, and in a city replete with temples, makes the connection between the temple as the dwelling of the holy God and the people who are in Christ as the very temple of this God.

Before Paul uses the temple metaphor, however, he introduces another image that paves the way for his point. In 1 Corinthians 3:5–8, Paul has used an agricultural metaphor to demonstrate the complementarity of his ministry and that of Apollos. He concludes by writing *we are God's servants, working together; you are God's field*, and then adds, *God's building*. The abrupt transition to *building* prepares for the temple metaphor. Paul's point is clear: 'the very image of a *building*, applied to the church, excludes individualism; it is not a single object but a corporate structure, a community.'[20] After making key points about the foundation of the building being in Christ and that the building has been constructed with appropriate materials by a craftsman, Paul switches to the Temple image. He writes in 1 Corinthians 3:16–17, *Do you* [plural] *not know that you* [plural] *are God's temple* [naos – singular] *and that God's Spirit dwells in you* [plural]? ... *For God's temple is holy, and you are that temple*. Collectively, the people of God are the temple, the *naos*, the shrine of God. By using the word that describes the temple building itself as distinct from the temple area [*hieron*], Paul focuses upon the holiness of the people and God's sanctifying presence in them.[21] The triune God dwells in and amongst his holy people as a people. This is unmistakable corporate and holy people of God language and offers a corrective to thinking that is all too often exclusively upon the indwelling of God in individuals. Paul's point is different. The people of God are the dwelling place of the holy and triune God who exists in unity and love.

Although both the NRSV and NIV translate the two uses of *phtheirō* in 1 Corinthians 3:17 as 'destroy' (*if anyone destroys God's temple, God will destroy that person*), Sampley makes a convincing case that the translation should be 'defile' in the first instance, and 'destroy' in the second, a clever play on words by Paul. If that is so, then Paul warns, *if anyone defiles the temple, God will destroy that one*.[22] The issue is not merely a question of disharmony within a sociological unit, however damaging that may be. Rather, this action defiles, that is, it affects the purity and holiness of the temple. This defilement renders it unfit for holy purposes and leads to its destruction.[23] Damage in relationships gives life to the contagion of sin – a point to which we will return in the last chapter.

This is also why Paul is so concerned later in the letter about the defilement that comes from participating in pagan temple meals. Anyone who eats at the table of a meal that is presided over by a god has become a partaker of that god and therefore has been defiled (1 Cor. 10:16–22). Such a one cannot be part of the table of Christ lest the contagion of defilement – the leaven of impurity – be introduced into the temple of God. Here Paul warns that anyone who destroys the unity of the people of God into which they are called and fashioned by the Spirit is defiling the dwelling place of God in his people – together.

The second point comes later. In 1 Corinthians 6:19, Paul asks the rhetorical question, *Or do you not know that your body is a temple of the Holy Spirit within you?* Here the context of 1 Corinthians 6:12–20 helps. Apparently some of Paul's converts consider themselves to be so spiritual that the physical body is of no consequence. Their logic seems to have run something like this. Salvation and sanctification are essentially spiritual matters, affecting the inner person. The body is material and therefore, as was commonly thought, essentially evil. It is 'fallen flesh', to use Paul's own language. Therefore, it doesn't really matter what happens to the body. Furthermore, it doesn't really matter what happens to my body and what I do with my body. That is none of your business.[24] They have taken Paul's teaching about 'all things are lawful' in a direction that is completely the opposite of Paul's view.[25]

The usual understanding of the situation against which Paul inveighs is a counter-cultural warning against the sexual mores of high-status men. Convention suggests that these men could have a variety of sexual partners that may include, in addition to his wife, a concubine, a mistress and prostitutes, male or female.[26] Bruce Winter[27] has sharpened this view by sketching an even more plausible background for this passage. According to Winter, the behaviour in 1 Corinthians 6:9–20 'is related to what ancient historians have designated 'the unholy trinity' of eating and drinking and immorality.[28] In Winter's view, the practices of the upwardly mobile in Corinth are reflected in this discussion. It was expected of young men when they assumed the *toga virilis* on reaching manhood that they would be part of a sort of 'coming of age' banquet, where the notion of 'food for the belly and the belly for food and the body for sex' would be put into practice.[29] In these 'coming out' parties, young men who had received the *toga virilis* as the right of passage not only to manhood but to riotous living, would use the services of high class prostitutes who plied their trade at dinners among the élite party-going set of Corinthian playboys.

Whatever the case, Paul rejects their continued acceptable of the cultural norms because it fails to understand some key points about the holy character of the new people of God. It is completely wrong-headed on three fronts, according to Paul. In the first place, the body does matter. Far from a 'don't care' attitude to the body, God cares greatly about it. We know that because he raised Jesus from the dead in bodily form.

Second, the physical body is important in holy living. Thus, 'with the statement τὸ δὲ σῶμα οὐ τῇ πορνείᾳ ἀλλὰ τῷ κυρίῳ Paul offers the believer a radical choice. This is more than a choice of behaviours: it is a choice of identities; a choice of which realm and which lordship one will dwell under.'[30] The Corinthians cannot be the holy people of God at the same time as they are being defiled by *porneia*.

But we need to go further. Paul's ethics are theological ethics not pragmatic moralisms. As May argues,

> To say that the believer's body is 'for the Lord' is not simply to say that the Christian identity has ethical implications. It is (as problematic as this may be) to speak of the believer participating bodily

in Christ. The Spirit dwells *in* the believer's body-as-temple. The body thus becomes holy ground, and owned by God. Similarly, the dreadful alternative, being 'for pornei/a', is not simply found in an unethical infringement of Christian norms, but is an alternative participation.[31]

In fact, according to Christine Hayes, Paul is the first to talk about contracting moral impurity from another person through sexual relations: 'No prior source emphasizes the notion of one partner to a mixed union contracting the moral impurity of the other.'[32]

Third, sleeping with prostitutes or engaging in casual sex is wrong because sexual intercourse is an act reserved for marriage (more on this topic in the next chapter). The consummation of the marriage covenant makes a man and woman into one flesh.[33] Sexual intercourse outside of marriage is more than an external recreational activity. It adversely affects the 'inner person'. Furthermore, we who are in Christ are part of his body and by sinning 'in the body' we are involving the body of Christ.[34] This drives Paul to say, *do you* [plural] *not know that your body* [singular] *is a temple of the Holy Spirit within you?* 'Like an exclusive sexual commitment, holiness as a sanctum for the resident Holy Spirit requires scrupulous fidelity and stewardship of the self as body properly set aside for the Spirit.'[35] They are therefore expected to glorify God in the body.

Paul's point here is that the dwelling place of God is in persons, whole persons, as well as the people of God corporately – God through his Spirit makes his temple within those who are part of his people. Paul combines the emphasis upon the people of God as a corporate entity with the personal. In both of these cases, Paul is making the same overall point – no one should damage the temple of God through defilement, either through destroying its unity or compromising its holiness. Anything which damages the person or the community disregards the fact that God has now made his dwelling in his people, corporately as the body of Christ, and in persons who take their existence from this corporate being.

Very few of those who would be called 'holiness people' will likely be involved in prostitution. Regrettable, casual sexual activity is another matter. Paul may well be addressing this approach to sexuality, not only because of his belief that sexual intimacy is to be reserved for those in covenantal union, but because this is a symptom of the cultural pressure on God's holy people. This pressure stands behind much of his discourse in 1 Corinthians.[36] This is an example of where they must be counter-cultural and marks the difference between a morality based upon 'what is the norm in society' and a Christian ethic that emerges out of theological foundations. Paul makes a similar case in 1 Thessalonians 4:3–8. Because 'the Thessalonian believers were no longer simply "Gentiles who do not know God," but now were members of the renewed Israel, the covenant people of God … they were to observe the boundaries of holiness that the new covenant marked out for them, whether in the area of sexual conduct or any other human activity.'[37] If that makes Paul's converts seem odd in society, so be it.

The concern for honouring God with our bodies is not restricted to sex, of course. And the appropriate fulfilment of sexual desires is not the only arena in which the holy people of God might be challenged to consider the importance of the physical body as the Temple of God. But for Paul, this is a particularly dangerous point of defilement which, together with idol worship, shows the thoroughly Jewish background of defilement, on the one hand, and the character of the holy people of God, on the other.[38]

3 Worship in Community: Discerning the Body

While Paul's temple metaphor is very important for the Corinthians because it reminds them that they are actually the dwelling place of the holy God, his most potent metaphor is the 'body of Christ' – they are the body of Christ. But if they know that they are the body of Christ, they have yet to understand its implication for life. And, once again, this finds its primary context in the appropriate worship of the holy God.

Paul reminds them that if they are to live as God's holy people, they must understand that they are all one in Christ and that this determines their identity. Paul writes, *in the one Spirit we were all baptised into one body – Jews or Greeks, slaves or free – and we were all made to drink of one Spirit* (1 Cor. 12:13). This is not the first time that Paul states this or something very similar (see Gal. 3:28). But here it emerges out of Paul's description of the body of Christ and shows the close connection between the corporate identity of God's people and the sacraments of Baptism and the Lord's Supper. Aspects of Paul's underlying beliefs about God's holy people are illuminated by considering these sacraments in 1 Corinthians.

3.1 Baptism

Paul takes it for granted that baptism signals or effects the incorporation of people into the body of Christ (see Rom. 6:1–4). It follows that God's holy people are all part of the one body of Christ, whether they are Jews or Greeks, slaves or free. For Paul this is important. And it cuts two ways. First, there are not two peoples of God – there is only one. The new covenant people of God, the Gentiles in Corinth, are descendants of the old covenant people of God who are *our ancestors* (1 Cor. 10:1). Paul has a conviction throughout his epistles that his Gentile converts constitution 'a part of renewed Israel—a vital portion of the covenant people of God—and as such had come into the realm of both the blessings and the challenges of that new status'.[39]

This is more than literary rhetoric for Paul – it is a theological axiom. To explain, Paul evokes the Exodus[40] and wilderness story, using the explicit term 'baptised' to describe their experience: *all were baptised into Moses in the cloud and in the sea and all ate the same spiritual food and all drank the same spiritual drink* (1 Cor. 10:2–4a). In other words, Paul believes that their ancestors were *'initiated into* the corporate experience of the *visible community* of the people of God'[41] through the redemptive activity of God and his care for the people in the wilderness. 'Baptised into Moses' is used as a metaphor of God's gracious incorporation of Israel into 'the privileges and blessings of the redeemed covenant people of God'.[42]

Paul then makes a completely unexpected assertion. Their ancestors in the faith are one with them, his Corinthian Gentile converts, because *they drank from the spiritual rock that followed them, and the rock was Christ* (1 Cor. 10:4b). Just in case they didn't get the point, he states that some of their ancestors were putting Christ to the test (1 Cor. 10:9). This language has puzzled commentators for centuries.[43] In fact, the simplest way of understanding Paul's language is probably what Paul has in mind: 'Christ was really a part of Israel's history.'[44] Paul thinks of God's salvific work in and through his people as a continuity.[45] It is also why he can speak of our election in Christ *before the foundations of the world to be holy and blameless before him in love* (Eph. 1:4). Whatever we might think of Paul's use of Numbers 20:1–13, it is clear that being 'in Christ' is the identification of the people of God, old or new.[46]

The second point, however, is that the life and experience of their ancestors in this instance serves as a pattern and warning to the new people of God in Corinth. Incorporation into God's people does not guarantee safety nor protect against falling into sin. Partaking of the same spiritual food and drink did not prevent their ancestors from falling into sin. Paul may well be alluding to the sacraments here. If so, then the point is clear: the sacraments are not magical. If not, the warning remains clear: do not be presumptuous in your response to God's grace. The lessons from the past need to be heeded: they are to avoid the same pitfalls and live holy lives. And that demands that they be counter-cultural whenever holy living might be in danger of being compromised.

But what triggers Paul's concern? The Corinthians have asked about eating meat offered to idols. Paul answers this question at one level (1 Cor. 8, inserts a fairly lengthy digression [1 Cor. 9:1 – 10:13]), then answers an underlying but unspoken question about Christian participation in pagan cultic practices.

It is not just eating food offered to idols that attracts Paul's attention. On the one hand, he holds that idols have no real existence (see 1 Cor. 8:4–8; 10:19). On the other, he sees huge dangers for his converts if they participate in pagan activities. Idolatry is a threat. Once again, the juxtaposition of an allusion to the Old Testament with the social context in Corinth helps us to see about what Paul is concerned.

Paul alludes to Exodus 32:1–6, the story of the Israelites and the Golden Calf, a well known, scandalous episode in Israel's story. Exodus 32:6 summarizes in these words: *the people sat down to eat and drink, and rose up to revel.* This polite summary of the event points to what some scholars call an orgy. Paul certainly thinks 'revel' (NRSV) refers to sexual immorality.[47] In the words of Thiselton, 'the combination of "lifting the lid" of control or restraint, fired by drink, a party mood, and the absence of the patriarchal figure of Moses led to more than mere *play.'*[48] This sets off alarm bells for Paul. He sees the same potent mix of religion, feasting and sexual licence in the festivals for the gods in Corinth. Idolatry mixes with *porneia* to bring defilement to the holy people, God's temple. In his view, these idolatrous cultic festivals were orgies of excess in the (already noted) unholy trinity of eating, drinking and fornicating.[49] If we are to understand Paul's point here, Thiselton tells us that we need to 'grasp fully the intimate connection for the LXX, hellenistic Judaism and Paul between worshipping religious constructs of human devising and sexual immorality and abandonment of the "censor" to sheer unbridled indulgence'.[50] Here seems to be Paul's concern – the extravagant, out-of-control, religious context of this lifestyle. Paul's point is this. If you think that being part of the people of God, recipients of his grace and full participants in the sacraments of the Lord protects you from the consequences of your behaviour, think again. Idolatry of any sort has consequences.

All of this has an uncannily contemporary ring. In any trendy part of my own home city and – doubtlessly – countless others, on any given weekend, a similar lifestyle is on display. Our gods are not idols of wood and stone – we're far too sophisticated for that, we think – but they are human constructs nevertheless. The cultic context of this lifestyle in Corinth makes Paul very concerned about the effect this has on the body of Christ. Once again, it defiles the body of Christ: *you cannot drink the cup of the Lord and the cup of demons. You cannot partake of the table of the Lord and the table of demons* (1 Cor. 10:20). He goes to great lengths to help the Corinthians understand what they have as yet only dimly perceived. The freedom they have in Christ must be exercised in the context of love for one another (see Gal. 5:13–15). They are one body – and everything they do affects the body because they are part of it. For Paul, even cultic excess in the community's worship faith beyond reasonable bounds is not to be practiced, *for God is not a god of disorder but of peace* (1 Cor. 14:36b). The physical body matters – because it is part of the body of Christ. Incorporation through baptism into God's holy people inevitably issues in a 'conversion of the imagination'[51], a changed worldview.

3.2 *The Lord's Supper*

As far as Paul is concerned, participation in the Lord's Supper is about more than a memorial to the Lord's death, important though that may be. For too many of us, the celebration of the Lord's Supper is less significant than it might be. Not so Paul. He devotes a lengthy section of this epistle to correcting the inappropriate behaviour flowing from his readers' deficient understanding of the nature of the celebration and of the body of Christ. In order to see the importance for Paul, we need to give some attention to the social context behind his instructions.

The whole notion of a cultic meal is a 'nearly universal phenomenon as part of worship in antiquity'.[52] Meals in temple precincts are a regular part of city life. Frequently these meals are explicitly cultic, or, have cultic overtones in which a god was thought to be present as the host. Cultic meals were almost certainly part of the worship of the new Christian community as well. These meals would have been held in the house church context of Corinth and, therefore, are affected by the everyday life of the people. But instead of being a table of the Lord, the Corinthians have made it into something rather different. So, what is happening in Corinth?

Paul's comments on the Lord's Supper begin at 1 Corinthians 11:17, not 11:23, and they begin with a stinging rebuke. The table, says Paul, is fostering *schisms* (1 Cor. 11:18) and *factions* (1 Cor. 11:19). Quite possibly the actual house church context is contributing to the problem. Perhaps the friends of the host are being invited to eat in the dining room, while the others would be invited to eat in the less favourable conservatory. Perhaps the rich are eating and drinking before the poor. Perhaps, as Peter Lampe has suggested,[53] we have separate sittings for those who arrive early and another for those who are later. Perhaps the powerful people who gather in the house church to celebrate the Lord's Supper are being waited upon by their servants, members of the large class of household slaves. Other household slaves are only able to arrive once their domestic duties are finished but by this time, the meal has already been consumed and too much wine has been drunk.[54] Dunn, citing Gill, observes that if the famine of AD 51 has affected Corinth, the problem of hunger is exacerbated, with the wealthy able to get scarce provisions.[55] Whatever the details, the outcome is clear: their celebration is actually fracturing the body of Christ – precisely in the sacrament which most clearly is intended to celebrate the unity.

Paul's concern seems to be that they are in danger of partaking unworthily, eating and drinking *in an unworthy manner* (1 Cor. 11:27 – *Hōste hos an esthiē ton arton ē pinē to potērion tou kuriou anaxiōs*). Clearly, Paul sees two ways of partaking unworthily: failure to discern the body and failure to examine oneself.[56] In the history of the church, emphasis has been given to one or the other of these warnings.

First, some believe that to profane the bread and cup of the Lord refers to the sanctity of the actual elements of bread and wine (in Orthodox, Catholic and Anglo-Catholic traditions, for instance). Therefore, great care is taken to preserve the sanctity of the 'host', the real presence of Christ.[57] Others take this to refer to the whole solemn occasion itself. Hence, the emphasis upon self-examination is very common in some Protestant traditions – 'let a person examine herself or himself'. On this view, the eating and drinking of the elements has an effect of health and wholeness, or destruction and disease, depending upon the spiritual state of the recipient (see 1 Cor. 11:30). This interpretation arises especially where there is little or no liturgical framework for the Eucharist, so that Paul's words are the sole (or main) point of liturgy and almost *always* taken out of their context within 1 Corinthians 11:17–31.

While the sacredness of the meal is never to be taken for granted, Paul's emphasis seems to lie elsewhere. On this view, 'discerning the body' is focused upon the *people* as the body of Christ rather than on the *elements* that are used in the communion service. Therefore, if one has a proper discernment of the body of Christ, the holy communion is a sacred communal meal which precludes independent and selfish action which does not take account of the body of Christ.

Paul thinks that the Corinthians are in grave danger here and it leads to a sharp warning: they are failing to *discern the body* when they eat and drink together (1 Cor. 11:27–31).

In some senses, these two lines of interpretation are complementary. An abuse of the 'body' is an abuse of Christ himself. The attitude and conduct of the Corinthians should be appropriate to the message. To fail to discern the body of Christ in the people for whom he died is tantamount to profaning the body of Christ in the bread. Thiselton argues that they are to be 'held accountable for the sin against Christ of *claiming identification with him* while using the celebration of the meal *as an occasion for causal enjoyment or status enhancement without regard to what sharing in what the Lord's Supper proclaims*'.[58] Again, Paul addresses a community issue from a profoundly theological centre, namely, the unity of the people of God in Christ (1 Cor. 11:28). The selfish behaviour of the Corinthian rich and status conscious is 'polluting the Eucharist' which means that its holiness is being infringed. 'The abusers have privatized their faith and their worship', notes Sampley; 'they have lost any sense that love as the right relation to others is the proper and necessary expression of their faith and the right relation to God.'[59] Paul warns them: 'the holy, when infringed, does not become ineffective, but rather its power for wholeness becomes a power of destruction (11:30).'[60]

In light of this, then, it is not surprising that Paul expects personal self-examination as an essential part of Eucharistic celebration (see also Matt. 18:15–20). When a believer partakes of the sacrament that celebrates one's continuing participation in the death and resurrection of Christ and mutual participation with others, it is appropriate to examine one's relationship with Christ as well as with others who are part of the body of Christ. That is why confession before one partakes of the Eucharist is an essential part of the liturgy in many traditions.

Three final points about the Eucharist. Paul writes earlier, *The cup of blessing that we bless, is it not a sharing in the blood of Christ? The bread that we break, is it not a sharing in the body of Christ?* (1 Cor. 10:16). Sharing the bread and wine is participation in Christ. He goes on, *Because there is one bread, we who are many are one body, for we all partake of the one bread* (1 Cor. 10:17). In this context, Paul is warning his readers that they cannot participate in the worship of idols because doing so is a participation in the fellowship of demons and that divided allegiance is a return to slavery.

For our purposes, the symbolism of the one loaf deserves further reflection. In many forms of the communion service, attention is quite properly directed to the broken bread as symbolizing the broken body of Christ. Paul, however, invites us to think about the loaf as a parable. Consider the loaf itself and the many pieces. Each individual piece of bread comes from the same loaf; each piece of bread is different. The symbolism is plain: the diverse members of the body of Christ have their origin and owe their very existence to Christ. In Paul's view, Christ is the creator of the community. Hence, believers do not individually gather together to create the church. The bread comes from one loaf and not the other way around. Believers owe their very existence to the one body of Christ; they derive their life and identity from Christ. That is the opposite of what many of us implicitly think, namely, that the body of Christ is made up of all the individuals gathered together. But this parabolic use of the loaf helps us show the folly of this anthropocentric rather than Christocentric understanding of the church, the body of Christ. The church is not a collection of individuals but the corporate body of Christ from which persons take their identity.

That brings us to the second lesson. Paul writes, *For as often as you eat this bread and drink the cup, you proclaim the Lord's death until he comes* (1 Cor. 11:26). The language of proclamation is critical: the Lord's Supper is a public proclamation of the gospel. It announces the good news that God in Christ is reconciling the world to himself through his sacrificial death on the cross. Because it is a proclamation of the gospel, it is not just for those who already are part of the gospel story. It is also an invitation to become part of the people of God. It is, in the words of the great Methodist scholar Vincent Taylor, an 'acted sermon … which represent[s] and provide[s] the opportunity for the spiritual appropriation of that which Christ made possible by His death.'[61] In that sense, it may become a 'saving sacrament', an invitation to become part of the people of God. Thus, for Paul, participation in the sacrament may be the opportunity for the seeking unbeliever to respond to the grace of God.

Third, we saw earlier that Paul insists that both slaves and free are part of the body. In Christ there are no distinctions. In this the church is to be radically counter-cultural; its agenda is not to be set by the prevailing society norms but by the reality of the new creation. God's holy people are to model his ultimate good purposes for his entire created order. Paul's instructions/response to the divisions are fairly clear: when they gathered, they are to be as God's people – no divisions in the community of faith are acceptable, whatever might be the case in society as a whole. And this is so, no matter how often text-proofing exegetes of scripture find biblical support for pernicious social barriers.[62]

Fee's views on this are strong: 'No "church" ', he writes, 'can long endure as the people of God for the new age in which the old distinctions between bond and free (or Jew and Greek, or male and female) are allowed to persist. [This is] especially so at the Table, where Christ, who has made us one, has ordained that we should visibly proclaim that unity.'[63] Paul's advice is this: the rich can have their parties at home. This is a celebration of the Lord's death and their mutual participation in his new covenant community, not a weekly party. Therefore, they ALL come together to focus on the gospel *story*, the proclamation of Christ's death and its corporate and relational consequences of their new existence in Christ's body (1 Cor. 11:33–34).

Paul would have little patience with those who excuse division on any grounds. It is difficult to see how the church can witness to the saving and sanctifying work of Christ through the Spirit while it continues to allow the sinful structures of this present and fast-passing-away age to determine its structures and practice.[64] God's holy people must be a holy community that reflects his holy purposes for the whole of his creation.

3.3 Because of the Angels

Paul's concern with the worship of the holy community extends beyond his discussion of the sacraments. The whole manner and intention of worship as it is practiced in Corinth needs attention because it is in danger of being centred on individual human performance rather than on God. Even their worship is in danger of being overwhelmed by prevailing and unexamined cultural norms. But they must remember that they are the dwelling place of the holy God. That must have implications for their corporate worship.

We have already seen how the desire for status and public affirmation may well have influenced some of Paul's converts to place special emphasis upon the public and spectacular gifts. In our previous discussion, we emphasized the need for love to be the controlling factor in the exercise of any gift within the community of faith. Paul's overriding concern in 1 Corinthians 14 is with the character of true spiritual and Spirit-inspired worship in the new community of faith.

The presence of the Spirit in their community is a given. When Paul is in dispute with the Galatians, he asks a series of rhetorical questions: *Did you receive the Spirit by doing the works of the law or by believing what you heard? Are you so foolish? Having started with the Spirit, are you now ending with the flesh? Did you experience so much for nothing?—if it really was for nothing. Well then, does God supply you with the Spirit and work miracles among you by your doing the works of the law, or by your believing what you heard?* (Gal. 3:3–5). Corporate worship is the context in which they hear the proclamation of the gospel and experience the presence and power of the Spirit.

At Corinth, however, this sense of the presence of God has been taken in a direction that alarms Paul. He has already guarded against importing a libertinism that comes from their culture into the community; one of his greatest concerns is that the worship of the community ought to reflect the very character of the God who is being worshipped, and whose very presence in their midst is known and experienced. 'This order in the nature of the God who acts coherently, faithfully and without self-contradiction should be reflected in the lifestyle and worship of the people of God.'[65] Hence, Paul argues that everything in Corinthian worship ought to be in harmony with the God of peace. But why is Paul so concerned to make this point?

One possibility is that Paul thinks that the worshipping community is actually participating in the heavenly worship around the throne of God. If that is so, the worship of the community is a sacred occasion in which the people of God join with the angels in worship of the triune God. This is almost certainly the perspective reflected in Revelation where the perpetual worship of God occurs. Even in the Corinthians' worship, however, the risk of compromise with the surrounding cultural norms that would contaminate, as it were, the purity of their worship, is real.[66] The worship of God's holy people is in the very presence of the holy God and is to reflect his character. This concern for purity in worship is also clearly the case at Qumran.

The Qumran community considers itself to be a spiritual temple, fulfilling the role that the hopelessly corrupt Jerusalem temple could not, including proper worship. They believe that 'in worship they were in communion with the angels ... [They are called upon] to join their earthly liturgy with that of the angels who worship with them.'[67] They are very conscious of the fact that their very worship is part of the worship offered to God by those angels of the presence surrounding God's throne. For Qumran, this includes the need for purification so that as worshippers they could take their place 'with the host of the holy ones, and can enter in communion with the congregation of the sons of heaven' (1QH XI = III 21b–22a). They worship 'in your [i.e. God's] presence with the perpetual host and the [everlasting] spirits'. They are actually in the presence of God, 'together with the angels of the face, without there being a mediator between the intelligent and your holy ones' (1QH XIV = VI 12b–13).

If this is so, it might cast light upon the much discussed phrase in Paul's contentious advice on head covering for women in 1 Corinthians 11:2–11.[68] In a much discussed piece of advice, Paul writes, *For this reason a woman ought to have a symbol of authority on her head, because of the angels* (1 Cor. 11:10).[69] The literature on the topic is extensive, not least because Paul does not go out of his way to explain why it is that he gives this advice, apart from the cryptic phrase: *because of the angels* (*dia tous aggelous* – 1 Cor. 11:10). What does Paul mean by this statement?

Perhaps the simplest suggestion is the best: the women are to cover their heads because the worship is in the context of the angels. However, that explanation still leaves the question unanswered about why the angels need to have the women's heads covered in their presence.[70] Two interesting and related points are attractive. Both of them quite rightly take for granted the fact that Paul is affirming the role of women in ministry in the community through his advice. In several key passages, Paul shows that within the people of God, men and women have an interdependent relationship (see 1 Cor. 7:2–4; Eph.

5:21–30). Paul knows that the Spirit has been given to the people of God without respect of gender.

But he is also concerned that the voice of women be heard in the community as the word of God and that they be given full authority in the community. Women who have been given the gift of prophecy are to exercise it for the upbuilding of the people of God. Francis Watson suggests that Paul advises women to cover their heads so that their voices can be heard free from the distortion caused by the erotic gaze.[71] Here the social context of the Corinthians might well have been influential in Paul's (Jewish?) solution to the problem.[72] But Watson further suggests that this solution is rejected by the Corinthians, who do not share Paul's Jewish cultural norms. Indeed, Paul invites the Corinthians to reflect on his advice (1 Cor. 11:13–16). Watson thinks Paul himself later realizes that veiling is not really the best solution to the problem.[73] Thus, in 2 Corinthians 3:12–18 he confines this actual veil, along with the metaphorical veil over minds of those who read Moses apart from Christ, to the old order. The veil is, after all, an inappropriate symbol of the new creation.

Another suggestion looks even more closely at the veil as a symbol of authority from the perspective of Paul's Jewish background. George Brooke[74] offers the intriguing suggestion that the veil (or embroidered cloth of some sort) as a symbol of authority might be illuminated from a Qumran text (4Q270 7 I, 13–15). In this text, the term *rwqmh*, which has resisted an agreed translation, probably refers to some sort of embroidered material since the word is used elsewhere in a similar fashion. This text includes a ruling on levels of punishment to be meted out in the community for murmuring against fathers and for offences against mothers. Two levels of punishment are set. The tariff for offences against the fathers is higher than for those against the mothers 'on the basis that the mothers do not have *rwqmh* in the midst of the congregation (*'dh*)'.[75] The meaning of the term in this context seems to be that the mothers 'are not permitted wear a mark of authority in the congregation'.[76] Brooke also reminds us that at Qumran 'the presence of angels also prevents various groups of people from taking a full place in the congregation.'[77]

In light of this discussion, Brooke thinks this text and 1 Corinthians 11:10 might be mutually illuminating. The key point is 'authority' (*exousia*). At Qumran, women apparently do not wear the symbol of authority in the congregation because they are women. But Paul's picture is radically different. While at Qumran, 'the presence of angels restricted membership in the congregation, for Paul women can indeed take their place in the worshipping community, even in the presence of angels, providing they do so with their heads covered.'[78] The head covering, then, is the symbol of authority to participate fully in the worship of the community even in the presence of the angels. A modern example of wearing a symbol of authority might be the wigs worn by barristers and judges who are acting in British Crown Courts.

> In 1 Cor. 11:10, the authority a women must wear on her head, whether a veil or braided hair bound up, enables her to participate in the praying community in her proper place so that the worshipping angels are not compromised by any kind of unnaturalness … What is worn by a woman, in this case "on her head", is a sign of (her) authority.[79]

Paul makes this point, then, to show the sacredness of the community's worship in which the whole new people of God participate with all creatures in the worship of the triune God and in the divine presence. The specific advice can only be understood in the cultural context of the day; the significance of the advice in terms of the inclusiveness of the new people of God and the sacredness of worship in the divine presence remains.

4 Saints and Sinners in Community

When we first read Paul's salutation *to those who are sanctified in Christ Jesus, called to be saints* (1 Cor. 1:2), we do not expect what follows. Although Paul celebrates the grace they have received and the gifts they manifest, he is soon addressing serious issues. This is a church torn by divisions (1 Cor. 1:10–16). Tolerance in sexual practice has reached shocking proportions (1 Cor. 5:1–8). Believers are taking each other to court to make sure they get their rights (1 Cor. 6:1–8).[80] Some think they are so spiritual that what they do with their bodies is irrelevant (1 Cor. 6:12–20). The Lord's Supper highlights economic disparity rather than their oneness in Christ (1 Cor. 11:17–22). Spiritual gifts are used like pieces in a game of spiritual one-upmanship (chapters 12 and 14). All these problems and more are present in this community. Are these really 'the saints', the 'holy ones'?

In fact, the range and depth of these problems have led some to suggest that Paul has three groups in mind. On this view, those who are unbelievers are called the 'unspiritual' [*psuchikos*] people (1 Cor. 2:14). They are outside the people of God – their unbelieving friends and neighbours. Paul is not particularly hard on them because they really cannot grasp spiritual reality. Then there are two classes of believers – those who are the 'saints' (1 Cor. 1:2) who live holy lives. The other class are those whom Paul addresses as *people of the flesh, infants in Christ* (1 Cor. 3:1, *ōs sarkinois ōs nēpiois en Christō*). They are believers but are not really 'spiritual people' (*pneumatikoi*) because they have not moved on to maturity. Some have suggested the division is between 'carnal' (*sarkinos*) and 'entirely sanctified' Christians.

This view has its attractions. At a stroke it solves the problem of how Paul could have classified as 'saints' people who are still participating in the self-indulgence of Corinthian culture. Although they have been saved, they have not yet been cleansed from all sin nor does the Holy Spirit dwell within. So this letter is essentially to these people of the flesh – they are not yet the saints. They need to be sanctified, to be made holy.

But there are insurmountable difficulties with this view. Apart from 1 Corinthians 3:1, there is little evidence that Paul is only addressing a group within the Corinthian congregation. For Paul, there is only one body of Christ and all believers are part of that one body. Theologically Paul cannot imagine a Christian who does not have the Spirit (Rom. 8:9). On the contrary, these people 'do have the Spirit; they are part of the new age that God is ushering in. But ... they are acting just like those who do not have the Spirit.'[81] Any attempt to empty the force of Paul's language by saying 'the person may have the Spirit but does the Spirit have the person?' would leave Paul completely mystified. So, Paul reminds his readers that they are those *who were washed ... sanctified ... justified in the name of the Lord Jesus Christ and in the Spirit of our God* (1 Cor. 6:11). These people do not need to become Spirit people. They need to become who they already are in Christ through the Spirit.

But what happens when things go wrong in the community of faith? Quite probably, this is neither the first nor the only time that Paul addresses the problem of behaviour in the community of a kind that does not match identity. When Paul writes to the Galatians, we don't know exactly what is going wrong in these house groups. But he is already all too aware of the problems that can emerge in the church. In fact, he hints in Galatians 5:15 that things might not be all they should be in this community, a view which might be strengthened by the lengthy advice in Galatians 6:1–10, ending with the exhortation to *work for the good of all, and especially for those of the family of faith* (Gal. 6:10).[82]

Quite possibly Paul believes some of the actions and attitudes in the community are reflective of the life of the flesh. Although Paul does not always think of the flesh in a negative way, the works of the flesh (*ta erga tēs sarkos*) in Galatians 5:19–21 are clearly negative. Perhaps some are in danger of returning to a self-centred mindset and produce activity that is the opposite of the fruit of the Spirit. Whatever the specifics, we are all alert enough to know that *enmities, strife, jealousy, anger, quarrels, dissensions, factions and envy* (Gal. 5:20, 21) wreak havoc in the church at any time. If this were a modern church, the problems might well be expressed differently – how about *my* rights, *my* happiness, *my* security, *my* family, *my* feelings, *my* pain? – but they would all still be manifestations of the self-centred mindset. And Paul reminds us that the consequence of selfish living and attitudes is 'corruption', personal and communal disintegration (Gal. 6:8a). That way lies destruction.

Paul does not leave the problem unaddressed, however. His advice is to the point: if anyone is detected in a transgression, you who have received the Spirit should restore such a one in a spirit of gentleness. Take care that you yourselves are not tempted. Bear one another's burdens, and in this way you will fulfil the law of Christ. Paul chooses his words carefully. This does not refer to persistent and arrogant transgression but probably alludes to some of the 'works of the flesh' that are damaging the community.

Paul, however, is more concerned with how to deal with the problem than the sin itself.[83] He reminds them that this is not the time for self-righteous condemnation, but an opportunity for the display of a spirit of gentleness, *en pneumatic prautētos*, a fruit of the Spirit. 'Paul is manifestly applying the basic principle of 5:25 and appealing for the exercise of meekness-and-gentleness (πραΰτης) … The Galatians' manner of life in the community, including their treatment of offenders, must be an outworking of their obedience to the Spirit.'[84] The antidote to such damaging behaviour is to remind them of the starting point – death to the life of the flesh – and to call them to live out the life of the Spirit in love to one another. They need to remember who they are, *hoi pneumatikoi*, the people of the Spirit. Most scholars agree with Martyn who states that this refers to 'the whole of the church, a community free from hierarchical distinctions. The Spirit leads members of the church to help one another not to stand apart from one another.'[85] The likely scenario, according to Dunn, is one in which the congregation seeks the leading of the Spirit. Then, one or more of those who detected the offender are led to deal with the case in question.[86] Thus, Paul's readers are to live like it through the Spirit, cooperating with the Spirit in producing the Spirit's fruit: if we live by the Spirit, let us also be guided by the Spirit (Gal. 5:25).

That does not mean, however, that Paul is unconcerned about blatant sin in the community. The case in 1 Corinthians 5:1–8, where *a man is living with his father's wife*, is condemned by Paul. This sin scandalizes those outside the church, yet, to his astonishment, is being applauded within the community. Paul condemns the Corinthians' tolerance of this defiling behaviour because of its affect on the whole community. This is a serious matter, but it is significant that Paul's expectations of discipline here is *for the destruction of the flesh, so that his spirit may be saved in the day of the Lord* (1 Cor. 5:5). Thus complacent acceptance of persistent sin in the community is destructive of the community and must be addressed for the health of the community and the salvation of the perpetrator.[87]

But these two examples leave us with a very uncomfortable question. How can these people whom Paul describes as 'people of the flesh' also be 'the saints'? And, if they are the holy ones, why are they acting in such dubious ways?

Paul thinks there are at least two reasons. First, they have failed to grasp the implications of the cross of Christ. The holiness of the people of God is grounded in and made possible by their full identification with Christ in his death and resurrection. In a compact passage in 2 Corinthians 5:21, Paul writes, *For our sake he made him to be sin who knew no sin, so that in him we might become the righteousness of God*. As we have already seen, when they were baptised into Christ, they were baptised into his death so that they might be raised to newness of life. This identification with Christ in his death marks the end of sin's rule in the believer's life. Not only are they set apart for God, they are actually called to live holy lives consistent with their calling. This God is holy and his people have been called to live lives that reflect his character. Their lives, both personally and as a people, are to reflect the holiness of God who makes his dwelling place in them.

They have also failed to grasp the strongly counter-cultural thrust of the gospel. This latter point is particularly important.

Paul's Corinthian converts live in a city and function in a culture with values that are often diametrically opposed to those of the people of God. But they are so steeped in their pagan culture that they are in danger of missing the message of the transforming power of the cross. Instead of grasping the full implications of what it means to be in Christ, they have squeezed the gospel into their societal norms and thereby distorted it.

For Paul, there is a fundamental incompatibility between a lifestyle that is indistinguishable from that of the surrounding culture and the life of God's holy people. 'The church's holiness demands that it really lives in accordance with the social order which God has given it, a social order which stands in sharp distinction to the pluralistic society in which it is located.'[88] Anyone who has not yet understood and internalized this is still an infant in Christ. Holy living is not an option for the saintly few but for all the saints. All who have been called by God to be his holy people are to be holy. There is no dual standard for believers as if there were some who are the sanctified and therefore live a holy life and others who are the saved but who continue to live as they always have.

In his recent magisterial commentary, Anthony Thiselton pointedly observes that

> with today's "post-modern" mood we may compare *the self-sufficient, self-congratulatory culture of Corinth coupled with an obsession about peer-group prestige, success in competition, their devaluing of tradition and universals, and near contempt for those without standing in some chosen value system. All of this provides and embarrassingly close model of a postmodern context for the gospel in our own times.*[89]

That thread has come through this discussion on holiness and community.

Paul's advice to his first readers about how God's holy people are to live in a context that is so often at odds with its own calling has an uncanny twenty-first-century feel. His reminder that the people of God, individually and collectively, are the very dwelling place of the holy God – a sort of walking temple – challenges any detachment of ethics from belief. These holy people are to glorify God in living lives that are counter-cultural in terms of unity in diversity, affirmation of the importance of the least in their society. Their participation in the sacraments celebrates their oneness in Christ even in their diversity; their community life together, centred on love, is to be the model of the new creation that God is inaugurating. Even their worship needs to be elevated to the place where they see themselves as participants in the perpetual heavenly praise being offered to God.

Paul's warnings about their behaviour and the defilement it brings suggests that sin is contagious. But Paul also indicates that holiness is to be contagious as well. We will look more closely at that theme in the final chapter.

Chapter Four

Holiness in the Real World

If holiness is to be anything more than personal piety, practiced only on Sunday and plagued by unattractive sanctimoniousness, it must be lived in the real world. This is a world of politics, power and people, full of ambiguity. It is a world in which the systems of evil threaten in an infinitive variety of insidious ways. This is our real world – it is also Paul's. In this chapter, we want to look again at our lives as God's holy people in this world.

1 Holiness and the New Creation

So if anyone is in Christ, there is a new creation: everything old has passed away; see, everything has become new! All this is from God who reconciled us to himself through Christ. So says Paul in 2 Corinthians 5:17–18a. Surprisingly, the phrase 'new creation' only occurs two times in Paul's writings.[1] But for Paul the new age has indeed dawned. God is doing a new thing (see Isa. 65:17). The new creation is underway. And this has profound implications for the path of Christian holiness.

1.1 New Creation and the New People of God

The usual place to start a discussion of new creation and Christian holiness would be with individuals. But that is not where Paul starts. He begins with God's action in Christ. His favourite phrase *in Christ* is participation language. And, as we have already seen, 'participation in Christ is irreducibly corporate'.[2]

The significance of this new creation solidarity is set out in Galatians 6:15. Paul writes, *For neither circumcision nor uncircumcision is anything; but a new creation is everything.* At this point, Paul has just about finished a rather heated letter to his Gentile converts. Apparently, some of them are considering being circumcised so that they could become full-fledged members of the Jewish community and thus true children of Abraham. But Paul wouldn't hear of it. His single focus is God's new creation in Christ. Paul's gospel announces a new reality which builds upon and includes the old, bringing it to its intended purpose. Therefore, as far as Paul is concerned, to be a true child of Abraham one has to identify fully with Abraham's seed, namely, Jesus Messiah. That identification no longer depends upon national identity, nor any other secondary distinction. God's new creation is solely through participation in Christ. In him God is creating a new people to be agents of his reconciling purposes.

This new people knows no human boundaries. Their new identity removes the blight of alienation between people and groups which plagues humanity apart from Christ. In Christ, the barriers of gender, racial identity and class are eliminated (Gal. 3:28). Thus, God's holy people make no place for racism, sexism or any other division manifesting the old way of living in Adam. They are part of a new people of God – *now* – and are done with old prejudices born of the distorted standards of this present age.

Care must be exercised, however. Paul is not arguing for the obliteration of diversity in the body of Christ, whether in terms of gifts, or cultural or national background. On the contrary, diversity is celebrated. In fact, as Campbell observes, 'being one in Christ rather demands difference since, if all were identical, there would be no need to seek for oneness or unity.'[3] He continues, 'thus whilst theologically, ethnic, gender and sexual issues are *relativized* by the call of Christ, they are neither *obsolete* nor *irrelevant* when it comes to real life situations.'[4] The point is, rather, that in this diversity, there is unity because all are one in Christ. The unity of all believers in Christ eliminates divisions based upon difference.

The clearest statement on this new identity is probably Ephesians 2:10–17. Paul (I concur with Bruce who stated that if Ephesians was not from Paul, it is the quintessence of Paulinism)[5] starts the passage by reminding his readers that *we have been created in Christ for good works so that we might walk in them* (v. 10). No escape from responsibility or hiding behind *not of works so that no one may boast* (Eph. 2:9): God's holy people live lives of service. Paul then describes the hopeless state of the Gentiles who were *without Christ, being aliens from the common-wealth of Israel, and strangers to the covenants of promise* (Eph. 2:12). The Gentiles and Israel are separated from each other – with the dividing wall being the hostility between Jew and Gentile. But, Paul says, that state of affairs has been brought to an end. God in Christ has *abolished the law with its commandments and ordinances, that he might create in himself one new humanity in place of the two, thus making peace* (Eph. 2:15). For Paul, there is only one people of God, not two, and it includes all reconciled to God and with each other in the one body. The new people of God is inclusive: the Gentiles are now *full participants with the saints and the household of God* (Eph. 2:19), having *access in one Spirit to the Father* (Eph. 2:18). All of this is accomplished, Paul says, through the cross – the means whereby God has reconciled *both groups to God in one body* (Eph. 2:16).

Reconciliation is the basis and sign of the new creation. The alienation that exists between people and symbolized by the intractable – still intractable – hostility between Jew and Gentile is over in the new creation. 'Alienation and division', says Beale, 'are no longer the rule in the new order in fulfilment of the Isaianic new creation prophecies.'[6]

1.2 New Creation and the New Person in Christ

Starting with the corporate people of God may have been slightly surprising; if so, we return now to more familiar territory.

Paul's language in 2 Corinthians 5:17–18b seems directed to individuals[7] – *So if anyone is in Christ, there is a new creation: everything old has passed away; see, everything has become new! All this is from God who reconciled us to himself through Christ* (2 Cor. 5:17). Thus, when we talk about the new creation as a people in Christ, it is also an intensely personal matter. The holy people of God is more than a collective for which one has a personal membership card. People who are incorporated into the new creation in Christ, the new solidarity in Christ, are also new creatures in Christ.

Paul thinks of a real change and this new creation is a present reality.[8] But some restrict the meaning of new creation language to the realm of future apocalyptic. On this view, new creation awaits the future, coinciding with the new heaven and new earth. For now, *kainē ktisis* is a kind of transit label attached to Christians in anticipation of the future resurrection or the coming of Christ when they will be a new creation. The guilty sinner will then be acquitted at the final judgement for the sake of Christ. For others, this future acquittal makes no substantial difference to the believer now. She or he is *clothed* in Christ's righteousness but not *made* righteous by God in Christ through the Spirit. Taken to its extreme, this view makes the new creation only a virtual reality, not a real change issuing in a new way of being.

Others suggest that, although the change is real and Christians are indeed new people, they are still engaged in a serious struggle within, 'not a conflict between the "old man" and the "new man", in which the "old man" may win out most of one's Christian life ... [but] with indwelling sin and sinful habit patterns.'[9] We have already shown why this is unlikely to be Paul's view. To be sure, the Christian

> still [faces] the flesh/spirit tension, for one still has a fallen body and thus experiences old bodily desires. There is also still temptation to act as if one ... [were] still the old person and part of the old order of things. The horror of sin for the Christian is that she or he may sometimes *choose* to act like what she or he is no longer – the

old person ... [But Paul also knows that] there is a new perspective because there is a new person. There is a transformed outlook because the person has been spiritually transformed.[10]

Paul's *thanks be to God through our Lord Jesus Christ* (Rom 7:25a) envisages a real change of allegiance to a new sphere of power, from the old way of self-centred being and orientation to the new God-centred and Spirit-led orientation, issuing in changed behaviour.

Moyer Hubbard is particularly helpful here. He argues that Paul is able to use the term *kainē ktisis* 'as an alternative formulation of his central Spirit affirmation – *the Spirit creates life'*.[11] Thus *kainē ktisis* in Paul as 'one of several ways in which Paul articulates the triumph of the Spirit over the flesh, and announces the decisive demise of the unenabled "old person" (Rom. 6:6)'.[12] But this new creation still awaits the resurrection of the body: our mortal bodies (*ta thnēta sōmata*) are still dead because of sin (Rom. 8:11). Nevertheless, the restoration is already underway. It is a *'pneumatological restoration'*.[13] In that sense, 'new creation refers to the new inner dynamic of the Spirit which has begun the process of restoring the *imago dei* marred by Adam's sin, and which enables those who rely on its power to fulfil the (true) requirement of the law (Rom. 8:4).'[14] And this is for all Christians, not just the more advanced. 'Paul is convinced that believers really are recreated in the inner person.'[15]

In Colossians 3:10–17, Paul develops the idea of transformation. This new self, says Paul, *is being renewed in knowledge according to the image of its creator. In that renewal ... Christ is all and in all! Therefore, as God's chosen ones, holy and beloved ... above all clothe yourselves with love, which binds everything together in perfect harmony. And let the peace of Christ rule in your hearts, to which indeed your were called in the one body.* Here Paul confirms that the focal point of the new creation is Christ who is all and is in all. The new creature is being renewed in the image of the Creator. Paul thinks of the people of God as the new humanity.

This is not, of course, to eliminate or even diminish the 'not yet' in Paul's thought. In the wider context of the new creation statement in 2 Corinthians Paul includes phrases which remind his readers about the present life of believers: *we have this treasure in clay jars, so that it may be made clear that this extraordinary power belongs to God and does not come from us* (2 Cor. 4:7); *We are afflicted in every way ... always carrying in the body the death of Christ* (2 Cor. 4:8, 10); *given up to death for Jesus' sake, so that the life of Jesus may be made visible in our mortal flesh* (2 Cor. 4:11). This kind of language continues in 2 Corinthians 4 and 5. In short, despite the powerful indwelling presence of the Spirit, transforming our lives in the present and guaranteeing our future (see also Eph. 1:13b, 14), Paul knows that all Christians still live in mortal flesh (see Rom. 8:23), in a fallen society (see Eph. 2:1–2), and in a context of spiritual hostility to God (see Eph. 6:10–13).[16]

Renewal in the image of the triune creator God points primarily to the restoration of damaged relationships. Paul thinks of this as an ongoing process with a beginning and a continuing outworking in the life of the believer and community. The key ingredient, of course, is love. So Paul says in Colossians 3:14, *and above all clothe yourselves with love.* It can be hardly incidental that the life of the triune God can be described as 'a perpetual movement of love'.[17] When love motivates attitude and directs action, the result is perfect harmony and the peace of Christ. To that extent the new people of God participate in the very life of the Trinity. They are new creatures, God's chosen and holy ones (Col. 3:12), bound together in harmony by the same love which is the life of the holy Trinity and experiencing the peace of Christ in the one body.

1.3 New Creation and the Created Order

We can all see the connection between new creation and renewed personal and corporate peace. But what can be said about the third consequence of the Fall, namely, the alienation of humankind from the created order? Does Paul have anything to say about the holy people of God and the environment?[18]

Some might suggest that this question is one that could only have been asked in a period when environmental concerns are before us every day. Christians, some might say, ought to be good stewards of the environment simply as responsible citizens but this does not emerge from any particular theological imperative. Paul's concern, thus, is with the salvation of people, and does not involve the environment; to argue for more is simply reading our own trendy green agenda back into Paul's thought. Besides, the fate of the created order is generally viewed as bleak – destruction to be followed by a new heaven and a new earth.[19]

But does that limitation on Paul's thought give adequate attention to the breadth of his mission and vision? Perhaps not. Jewett thinks that 'scholars have refrained from thinking through the implications of Paul's argument because they failed to take the missional context into account.'[20] According to 2 Corinthians 5:17–19, Paul notes that God's holy people, his new creation, are not simply reconciled to God; they are to be agents of that reconciliation in the world. They are to minister the peace of Christ and to model the love of Christ amongst their fellow human beings in the real world.

If the salvation offered in Christ is as universal in scope as Paul believes it to be, then God's big purposes must also include restoring the entire created order to its intended purpose. As agents of the reconciliation offered in Christ, his holy people are called to be agents of this wider reconciliation. Salvation 'cannot, almost by definition, be something merely individual or individualistic', writes Dunn. 'The "with Christ" cannot be fully enacted except as a "with others" and "with creation".'[21] On the contrary, a proper symbiotic rather than parasitic relationship with the rest of God's created order is the appropriate witness to the salvation we experience in Christ. 'In Christ we are restored to our full humanity as God's stewards of creation and shapers of culture.'[22]

Paul points in this direction in at least two passages. According to Colossians 1:15–20, salvation is 'a cosmic ... process of which individual salvation is only a part'.[23] Paul writes, *For through him [Christ] God was pleased to reconcile to himself all things [ta panta] whether on earth or in heaven, by making peace through the blood of his cross.* Paul not only sees the cross of Christ as effecting the reconciliation of humanity with God and each other; the same peace made by Christ on the cross is extended to *all things.* Without attempting to explain the means by which Paul sees this occurring, it is clear that God's plan of salvation is breathtakingly broad: people in Christ and the created order are all brought to their intended purpose through the salvation offered in Christ.

The second passage is worth quoting in full. In Romans 8:19–23, Paul writes, *For the creation waits with eager longing for the revealing of the children of God; for the creation was subjected to futility, not of its own will but by the will of the one who subjected it, in hope that the creation itself will be set free from its bondage to decay and will obtain the freedom of the glory of the children of God. We know that the whole creation has been groaning in labour pains until now; and not only the creation, but we ourselves, who have the first fruits of the Spirit, groan inwardly while we wait for adoption, the redemption of our bodies.*

Creation suffers as a consequence of human sinfulness. But this suffering also contributes to human suffering. Furthermore, in Paul's view, this distorted relationship between humans and creation is ongoing.[24] Just as Paul thinks that all humans replicate disobedience generation-by-generation so that all have sinned, the chaotic nature of creation in relationship to humanity is continuously replicated.

After a careful and detailed examination of Paul's intertextual sources in Romans 8, Laurie Braaten notes, 'Paul does not espouse a pessimistic view of the present creation which God feels compelled to destroy; rather, he speaks of the redemption of the present created order.'[25] Thus, when Paul speaks of the children of God in Romans 8:17 and their inheritance in Christ, creation itself is an important part of this inheritance. God's redemptive action for all people, Jew and Gentile alike, is seen 'within the context of God's salvific act for all creation'.[26] God's relationship with his created order, expressed first in the creation stories, then in the conclusion to the flood narrative and continuing in the series of covenant relationships culminating in the new covenant with his renewed people are all directed towards his ultimate good purposes for all, including the created order.

Nevertheless, the renewal of creation is an ongoing project that is both already and not yet. God's holy people see creation through different eyes. As people renewed in the image of the loving, creating, sustaining and redeeming God, our steward-ship of his world is to be carried out in the context of love and harmony, not exploitation and abuse. The saints care about the planet. And they do so *now*, sometimes in opposition to the principalities and powers (Eph. 6:12). Of course, 'Paul con-centrates on the transformed children of God rather than on specific actions and policies they may be led to follow in carry-ing on the ethic of transformation (Rom. 12:2); he assumes that the renewed mind of such groups will be able to discern what God wills for the ecosystem.'[27]

Thus we experience the presence of the Spirit in the body of Christ and live lives as new creatures in Christ *now*, even as we remain in mortal flesh and await the resurrection of our bodies. In the words of N. T. Wright, 'the challenge of holiness cannot be put off until some future date; nor can the challenge to bring all things in subjection to the saving rule of God's people, a task which must begin with inarticulate prayer and continue forward from there.'[28]

So creation itself waits in hope, along with the people of God, for the ultimate completion of God's good purposes. Mean-while, we live as resurrection people now: people of life, not death; of hope, not despair; of holiness, not defilement; in antic-ipation of the redemption of our bodies and the restoration of all things. This, too, fits into the purposes of God who calls his holy people to share in the ministry of reconciliation even as we await the glorious future when Christ shall be all and in all. 'Christians must be in the forefront of bringing, in the present time, signs and foretastes of God's eventual full healing to bear upon the created order in all its parts and at every level.'[29]

2 Holiness, Identity and Citizenship

According to Acts, Paul is a Roman citizen. Interestingly enough, we would have trouble deducing anything about this from his letters. He does, however, tell us quite a bit about his own Jewish background (see Phil. 3:2–6). Although he considers his Jewish heritage to be important, in comparison to the far greater privilege of knowing Christ, an impeccable Jewish pedigree is an irrelevance (3:8). That would probably have relieved his Gentile readers in Philippi.

For them, however, Roman citizenship would have been a different matter.[30] Philippi is a city with special status as a Roman colony where Roman citizenship is highly prized because of the status and privileges attached to it. Some of Paul's readers may well have been citizens of Philippi and Rome, provoking something of an identity crisis. Paul takes this problem seriously and reminds them that they are saints, God's holy people, because they are in Christ (Phil. 1:1). This is the language of belonging, of full identification with God's purposes. All who are in Christ have this new identity: *our citizenship*, says Paul, *is in heaven* (Phil. 3:20).

This is a powerful image in a political context in which Caesar is Lord and where privilege is attached to Roman citizenship. Rome is powerful, imposing its will and its own brand of law and order on a vast region. And this power has devastating effects upon the Mediterranean world. Beneath the ruins, roads and walls – so evident today across the Roman Europe as the remains of an advanced society – lay the sufferings, subjugation and degradation of countless people. Furthermore, as Robert Jewett observes, 'imperial ambition, military conflict, and economic exploitation ... led to the erosion of the natural environment throughout the Mediterranean world, leaving ruined cities, depleted fields, deforested mountains, and polluted streams as evidence of this universal human vanity. That such vanity, enhanced by the Roman civic cult, was promising the restoration of the "golden age" appears utterly preposterous.'[31] The impact upon the nascent Christian community should not be understated either. In fact, William Campbell has recently argued that 'the effect of imperial policies and power upon both "Christian" and Jewish communities is shown to have been much more significant in its influence upon the eventual formation of gentile "Christ" identity than might otherwise have been realized.'[32]

This metaphor of citizenship in heaven, then, strikes right at the heart of the identity of the proud citizens of Rome in Philippi. In bluntest terms, Paul reminds his readers that they have a higher loyalty to a far superior kingdom. This new identity relativizes all other loyalties although it does not obliterate them. Their calling as 'the holy ones', 'citizens of heaven' does not remove them from the real world. Rather, their calling 'takes place at a particular time and place and that status remains a given, an essential component of one's ongoing identity in Christ, subject only to the Lordship of Christ'.[33] But the Lordship of Christ affects all identities and takes priority over everything else. Christians, then and now, can never give ultimate allegiance to any state or system – nationalism and patriotism all too often drift into elitism, racism and even idolatry. Ultimate loyalty of believers can only ever be offered to Christ, who is Lord, not Caesar.

Allegiance to Christ has a profound effect on every aspect of life. That is why Paul calls his readers to *live your lives as worthy citizens of the gospel of Christ* (Phil. 1:27). This allegiance is particularly potent in situations when the imperial state arrogates power and authority to itself that is a parody of the Lordship of Christ and sovereignty of God. This picture forms the backdrop to much of the New Testament and is especially vivid in the Apocalypse. It also has an uncanny contemporary resonance. Dean Flemming writes, 'Wherever governments or global conglomerates fill their own coffers at the expense of powerless people; wherever political or commercial empires behave in ways that demand idolatrous allegiance; wherever nations use military, economic, or political coercion as a tool of self-serving policies; wherever societies or individuals embrace an ethos of greedy consumption – there is Babylon reborn.'[34]

This is Paul's context. Bochmuehl comments, 'Against the colonial preoccupation with the coveted citizenship of imperial Rome, Paul interposes a counter-citizenship whose capital and seat of power are not earthly but heavenly, whose guarantor is not Nero but Christ. Philippi may be a colony enjoying the personal imperial patronage of Lord Caesar, but the church at Philippi is a personal colony of Christ the Lord above all (2:10–11).'[35] Followers of Christ need to live as citizens worthy of the gospel in public as well as private spheres.

If the loyalty of the Philippians is to Christ, not Rome, old patterns of behaviour just won't do. This will only happen, however, if they embody the mind of Christ. Paul sets out for them what he means by the mind of Christ in a sublime passage in Philippians 2. Gorman[36] notes that the opening words of this passage are written against the background of the 'scriptural language of the divine image and glory and the competing Roman language of claims to imperial divinity. Thus Christ is like the God of Israel and is truly divine, unlike the emperor, who is a pseudo-god.'[37] Furthermore, Christ's actions are contrary to expectation: Roman gods just don't act this way (Phil. 2:7–8). They 'exercise power and privilege, seek status and honor, and perpetually "climb upward" as proofs of divinity; this "form of God" did just the contrary'.[38] Philippians 2, which is central to any biblical understanding of the incarnation, gives Paul's best example of how Christians are to live. The whole story of Christ's life, death, incarnation and exaltation is to be the pattern that they are to make their very own.

In the context of Roman hegemony, one can hardly imagine a starker contrast to state power than the story of Jesus. The fact that Jesus not only became human, became the servant of all (an echo of Mark 10:45, perhaps) but became obedient to death, even death on a cross (Phil. 2:5–8) would not be lost on those who treasured Roman citizenship. But because of his faithful obedience, God has exalted Christ to the highest place where he is Lord of all. This is Paul's controlling story and it is a story of love.[39]

Paul's readers are to let the mind of Christ be at work in their midst, fostering unity, mutual concern and support. Paul's desire is for community health that creates corporate solidarity and identity. Their public identity should not be of fractiousness but rather the 'behold how they love one another' of the Fourth Gospel. Once again, against the background of empire and the power of the state so clearly set out in this hymn of the incarnation, this kenotic kind of living becomes even more important. Wagner believes that 'Paul offers it to the Philippians as the foundational paradigm for "living as citizens in a manner worth of the gospel".'[40] Christ's example is to be the pattern of their lives: *let the same mind be in you that was in Christ Jesus.*

Paul sets this requirement out in terms of his own desire: *I want to know Christ and the power of his resurrection and the fellowship of his sufferings* (Phil. 3:13–14). To share in Christ's sufferings means to be called to have a lifestyle that conforms to the cross of Christ. This is intensely personal; it is equally corporate. It is therefore a lifestyle that characterizes individuals who are part of the people of God, and the communal life of the people of God both locally and beyond. People whose lives are conformed to Christ are not looking out for their own interests but the interests of others. They are not seeking their own advantage, but that of others; they are not concerned with their own status but consider all people in Christ to be in solidarity with them – fellow citizens of heaven. As Campbell notes, 'it was such a commitment to solidarity and mutual caring that enabled the Pauline communities not only to survive but to grow despite a hostile environment. Within these communities they belong to Christ and through him to each other.'[41]

Paul considers the fellowship in Christ's suffering to be a privilege, reflecting the holiness of God, not because suffering is good for its own sake but because it reflects who God is. In Gorman's words, 'the obedient Christ is exalted because in manifesting true *divinity* as the form of God taking the form of a slave (by becoming human and offering himself in death), he also manifested true *humanity* (unlike Adam) – as the obedient Son of the Father.'[42] It also entails the hope of sharing in the vindication of Christ by God who has exalted him to the right hand. Because we share in the fellowship of his sufferings, we also share in the hope and power of the resurrection for the future. 'Salvation for Paul ... is the sovereign gift of God in Christ which is accepted by faith alone and then concretely *embodied* in the banal, sublime and excruciating realities of the believer's life – by "the power of his resurrection and the fellowship of his sufferings".'[43]

Is such obedience possible? In a passage that has often puzzled his readers, Paul writes, *Not that I have already obtained this or have already been perfected ... Let those of us then who are perfect be of the same mind* (3:12–16). The problem arises because of Paul's use of 'perfected ... perfect' in apparently contradictory ways. In the first instance, he states that he has not yet been perfected. In contrast to those who may claim perfection, Paul realizes that he is still in the process of knowing Christ and being conformed to his image. By looking at the unveiled glory of Christ he is being *transformed from glory to glory* (2 Cor. 3:18). But Paul knows that a claim to perfection, whether by his near contemporaries at Qumran or modern 'sinless perfectionists', would simply be down to defining holiness in terms of performance targets and meeting them. Once Paul might well have claimed such performance himself – *as to the law, blameless* – but now that he knows Christ he realizes that perfection is not about performance. Perfect performance would simply be another way of *having a righteousness of my own that comes from the law, [rather than] one that comes through faith in Christ* (Phil. 3:9). Only in the light of Christ's obedience and Paul's single-minded allegiance to Christ can he state, *Let those of us then who are mature* ['perfect'] *be of the same mind.* 'Paul's life replicates the pattern of Christ's only because Paul has been united with Christ.'[44]

Thus Paul expects an embodiment of holiness *now* in corporate as well as personal terms. So he urges them to *work out your own salvation with fear and trembling* as well as reminding them that *it is God who is at work in you, enabling you both to will and to work for his good pleasure* (Phil. 2:12). 'Paul addresses his exhortation and teaching in Philippians not to isolated individuals, but to individuals in community. As the Philippians work out their own salvation, they do so as a community.'[45] Paul expects them to live as citizens of heaven. As citizens of heaven, they are often counter-cultural. They are to be *blameless and innocent, children of God without blemish in the midst of a crooked and perverse generation* (Phil. 2:15). So, Paul writes, *this one thing I do ... I press on toward the goal for the prize of the heavenly call of God in Christ Jesus. Brothers and sisters, join in imitating me, and observe those who live according to the example you have in us* (Phil. 3:17).

3 Holiness and Eschatology

All of that brings us inexorably to the big question of holiness and eschatology: 'how holy are God's people called to be in the present as they await the consummation of all things in Christ'? It's the question that has been a backdrop to this whole conversation and has received diverse answers from students over the years. Eschatology is popularly defined as 'the doctrine of last things'. But if biblical eschatology is the direction and goal of God's active covenant faithfulness in and for his created order, eschatology does not just refer to the final goal but also includes the way in which God's good purposes are being accomplished in the present.[46]

Because of Christ, as Paul now understands it, the future is already occurring in the present.[47] To be sure, the present age still continues. Or, as Richard Hays puts it, it is like 'finding ourselves within an unfinished plot line'.[48] Hence, Paul's eschatology is characterized by a tension between the already and the not yet. This 'between the times' experience of the people of God runs like a thread in all of Paul's theology.

3.1 May the God of Peace himself sanctify you entirely

One of Paul's clearest calls for Christian holiness comes in 1 Thessalonians 5:23–24: *Now may the God of peace himself sanctify you entirely, and may spirit, soul, and body be kept sound and blameless at the coming of our Lord Jesus Christ. The one who calls you is faithful and he will also do it.* The text, however, raises important questions. What does Paul mean by 'blameless' and how does it relate to his understanding of Christian holiness? Is this a term relating to human behaviour or is it descriptive of the believer's standing in Christ? Does Paul think that this is the goal towards which his readers are called but one which will be realized only *at the coming of our Lord Jesus Christ* or is this a prayer which is now to be answered in the life of the community of faith?

Paul sets out the context by reminding his Gentile readers[49] that they have received 'eschatological salvation from imminent divine judgment'.[50] These converts, have *turned to God from idols ... to wait for his Son from heaven ... who rescues us from the wrath that is coming* (1 Thess. 1:9–10). But conversions based upon hope for the future with no effect on the present are often superficial and the effects short-lived. What is needed is a new community and a new identity in which the hope can be fostered. So Paul reminds them that they are now to embody the ethic of the holy people of God by being, as Johnson terms it, an 'eschatological instantiation of Israel configured around a crucified Lord'.[51]

This life, in Paul's view, always includes suffering (1 Thess. 3:3–4), not only in imitation of their fellow believers or of Paul but of Christ. Paul holds that 'being a follower of Christ means sharing in his sufferings; and dares to suggest that, precisely because they are Christ's sufferings, they can bring life and comfort to others.'[52] This does not refer primarily to a once-off conformity to the image of Christ who is the image of God. Rather, 'likeness to God for the Christian disciple in Paul's thought world entails continual participation in the death of Jesus Christ. It means being, in an unrighteous world, righteous as God is.'[53]

Much of the material in the Thessalonian epistles is devoted to the theme of the coming of Christ. Two points are important. First, Paul denies that a timetable can be set (1 Thess. 5:1–2). Instead Paul shifts the focus to their lives as Christ's representatives in the present. So he reminds his readers about what they know already because, as he puts it, *you yourselves have been taught by God to love one another: and indeed you do love ... But we urge you, beloved, to do so more and more, to aspire to live quietly, to mind your own affairs, and to work with your hands, as we have directed you, so that you may behave properly toward outsiders and be dependent on no one* (1 Thess. 4:9–12). Christ's return may be imminent but love is to continue to be the mainspring of the community's life. And that means mutual support within the community and a clear witness to those outside.

The second point is subtle, but also important. Paul likely numbers himself among those who would remain alive at the coming of the Lord. That shifts the emphasis in Paul's exhortations to living *now* in light of the parousia, clearly helping to nuance Paul's thought in 1 Thessalonians 3:12 and 5:23.

3.2 Blameless

Paul uses the term 'blameless', a term connoting integrity, not flawlessness, three times in 1 Thessalonians. The phrase, 'blameless at his coming', has significance for both the character as well as the timing of 'entire sanctification'.

The first instance in 1 Thessalonians 2:10 follows a lengthy discussion of the missioners' impeccable behaviour. Everything they did amongst the Thessalonians was open and aboveboard. Paul and his colleagues are motivated solely by their desire to share the gospel with integrity because they love the people (1 Thess. 2:8). Here we see clearly the combination of motivation with action. Pure motivation issues in behaviour with integrity. The term 'blameless' is the last of three terms chosen to describe their life among the Thessalonians: *holy, upright and blameless*. Marshall suggests that 'the three adjectives (representing three Greek adverbs) are close in meaning and are put together for emphasis ... [The final one, *amemptos*] **blameless** refers to conduct which is free from any accusation that it falls below the standard of justice (5:23).'[54] In sum, the term here points to the complete integrity of their conduct before the Thessalonians and its transparency before God.

The second use occurs in 1 Thessalonians 3:13, where Paul prays that God might establish their hearts *blameless in holiness*.

In the first part of the prayer Paul wishes that *the Lord would make you increase and abound in love for one another and for all, just as we abound in love for you* (1 Thess. 3:12). The bond between love and holiness is made explicit here. As Best notes, 'love and holiness are not in our context two virtues among other virtues but are umbrella words for the whole of Christian activity.'[55] Love is the very hallmark of Christian existence. Now Paul prays that the love they have already been given through the Spirit will go on increasing and growing.[56] Andy Johnson draws attention to the *'reciprocal movement* of Paul's prayer. The movement from being engaged in grace-enabled self-giving practices *to* the establishment of their hearts/imaginations as blameless in holiness at the parousia.'[57] Indeed, for Paul the ethical imperatives of holy living are all connected to God's love as the central motivation in their lives.

Paul clarifies the significance of love for ethics in the next section (1 Thess. 4:1–8). When Paul describes God's purposes for their lives, he says *this is the will of God, your sanctification* (1 Thess. 4:3). He then follows this immediately with a command *that you abstain from sexual immorality.* This is a new church. Consequently, it is possible that 'as new converts from paganism, some may not have broken completely with their former pattern of life'.[58] Paul may have been taking pre-emptive action by telling them that 'sexual purity is a specific manifestation of the general holiness of life demanded of God's people.'[59] He becomes much more explicit about sexual immorality later in 1 Corinthians 5 and 6 where sexual impurity defiles the people of God, the body of Christ and the holiness of God's people.

Holy living cannot, however, be reduced to sexual purity. Rather, Paul grounds it upon the premise that no one should exploit a brother or sister. Once again, love is central. Genuine love, the love of God poured out in our hearts by the Spirit as opposed to self-centred love does not exploit the other person (see 1 Thess. 4:3–8). That is why holiness, centred on love for God and neighbour, is incompatible with sexual promiscuity: *for God did not call us to impurity but in holiness* (1 Thess. 4:7).[60] Blameless living, then, comes from the presence in their lives of the grace of God through his love poured out in their hearts, daily increased by the Lord himself. In turn, the believers are committed to live according to the demands of love. 'True blamelessness in word and action must be the fruit of inner sanctification.'[61]

3.3 At the coming of our Lord Jesus

But just when does Paul expect them to be *blameless in holiness*? Some have argued that the phrase *at the coming of our Lord Jesus* means that Paul prays that his readers will be made blameless in holiness *at* the parousia or even made blameless in holiness *by* the parousia.[62]

Two points may help us decide. First, Paul has already prayed that the Lord would increase their love. This prayer is for the present time, not for an increase in love at the parousia. It is this present supernatural gift of superabundant love which leads to the establishment of their *hearts in holiness*. 'Therefore', as Bruce comments, 'to love as Paul desired his converts to love would result in their living sanctified lives, placing them beyond any opprobrium at the judgment.'[63] The parousia is not the centre of God's saving work in Christ for humanity. That could only be the cross and resurrection for Paul. All salvation, initial as well as entire sanctification, is founded upon God's work in Christ.

Second, as noted above, Paul thinks that the coming of Christ will be sooner rather than later. The importance of this perspective can hardly be overestimated even if it has not been sufficiently recognized. Paul expects blameless living now because he expects the parousia at any moment. 'Implicit here and throughout the epistle is the conviction that the holy life is not just a future possibility but must be a present reality.'[64]

So, when does Paul expect this to occur? As Ernest Best notes, 'the second half of the verse reiterates the first chiastically and at the same time amplifies it, identifying the moment at which complete holiness is essential, the parousia; holiness, of course, will not come suddenly into existence then unless they are now already "holy" (the saints) and seeking holiness.'[65] This is clearly Paul's concern. He is not praying for a post-mortem holiness for some and a last gasp holiness for others. Not only does he expect most to be alive at the parousia; he believes that they should be ready now for the parousia which could come at any time: *the Day of the Lord will come like a thief in the night* (1 Thess. 5:2). Paul's prayer is that 'their converts may be preserved entirely without fault *until* the Parousia and be so found *at* the Parousia, when they will be perfected in holiness'.[66]

This is not a matter of personal or corporate achievement, however. Nor is it simply the fact that they are adjudged to be holy because 'in Christ' they are holy, whatever their lives are like. Paul would not be wasting his words urging them to live holy lives if that were the case. Although believers themselves cannot produce that holiness of heart that is the motivational centre of the holy life, blamelessness cannot be achieved without the response of believers. Paul is quite clear on the source and effectual power behind Christian holiness: *The one who calls you is faithful, and he will do it* (1 Thess. 5:24). Paul clearly echoes the Old Testament call by God for a holy people, a kingdom of priests and a holy nation. They are sanctified by God (Lev. 20:8; 21:8) and are to sanctify themselves (Lev. 11:44; see 2 Cor. 7:1). This is exactly what the saints in Thessalonica are to be, not merely *de jure* but *de facto*. And Paul also believes that the God who calls his people to holiness before him and in the world is the faithful covenant God who will sanctify them entirely (1 Thess. 5:23). In short, 'They are holy, they need to strive for holiness (1 Thess. 4:3) and God alone can produce holiness in them.'[67]

4 Contagious Holiness

We come finally to the notion of contagious holiness. Although it could have come earlier in the discussion, it actually underpins everything that has been said about God's holy people in this world – we are called to be contagious.

Sin, too, is contagious. That seems to be behind the concern Paul has about sinful behaviour in the body of Christ as we saw earlier. The issue comes to a head in the story of tolerated incest in 1 Corinthians 5, the first in the 'series of problems where the standards of the world and its acceptance of such persons have wrongly come over into the community'.[68] The reasons why are probably quite complex. Most persuasive is the view that the flagrant offender is a high-status person in the community.[69] Paul is not impressed (see 1 Cor. 5:2). The sin in their midst is affecting the whole body. Behind Paul's concern is the corrosive effect of sin in the community. Paul insists, therefore, that they are to expel the person so that the purity of the body of Christ might not be compromised.

This point, of course, could be easily misunderstood. The Corinthians think that Paul means they should cut themselves off from their unbelieving neighbours – become separate from the world – in order to preserve their holiness. But Paul's point is different. Tolerating blatant sin in believers infects the whole community of faith. It is covenant destroying, a bit like the betrayal of a spouse that only shows up when disease strikes the unsuspecting partner.

Unbelievers, on the other hand, are the focus of God's love and concern. Paul's missionary activity depends upon this love and concern. If the believing community were to be cut off from *the immoral of this world,* it would abort the mission of God to the Gentiles. In fact, Paul is not particularly concerned about contact with the contamination of sin when it is in the context of mission.

The reason for this is Paul's confidence that holiness is also contagious and that the holiness of the people of God is greater than the impiety and godlessness of the world. Although Paul does not report directly on the practice of Jesus, nor does he give much evidence of using Jesus' teaching directly,[70] he is likely very well informed about the good news proclaimed and enacted by Jesus. If this is so, then Paul follows the re-definition of holiness modelled and taught by Jesus. Compassion for the lost, healing for the diseased, rescuing the dispossessed, reintegrating the excluded – these define the mission of the Holy One of God and his people. Holiness triumphed over impurity in the ministry of Jesus – this seems to be Paul's view as well. Holiness is contagious.

In a fascinating passage, Paul writes, *For the unbelieving husband is made holy through his wife, and the unbelieving wife is made holy through her husband. Otherwise, your children would be unclean, but as it is, they are holy* (1 Cor. 7:14). Although we cannot discuss all the implications of this passage here, the main point for our purposes is this. The holiness of believers through the indwelling of the Holy Spirit has an affect on their spouses and children. The holy people of God live lives of contagious and transforming love. Although this seems extraordinary, on closer examination it coheres exactly with Paul's core belief in the redeeming character of God's love, on the assertion that this love has been poured into the hearts of believers, and that the community is called to be agents of this reconciling love of God. 'As surely as sin's power is lethal, even more so is God's power evident in those who belong to God.'[71]

The conclusion to be drawn from this is clear and challenging. Christian holiness is not primarily about separation at all. The community of faith, God's holy people, are not called to holy separation and isolation from the world, but to holy mission and holy love in the world. God's holy people are to be agents of God's transforming grace in all the circumstances in which they are placed.

Contagious holiness. In the intimacy of nuclear family, in the fellowship of believers, in the brokenness of alienated societies, in the face of exploitative scarring of the natural environment – these are the places where the contagious holiness, the holy love, of God's holy people about which Paul speaks is active in God's big purposes for his entire created order. This is holiness in the real world.

Select Bibliography

Adewuya, J. Ayodeji, 'The People of God in a Pluralistic Society: Holiness in 2 Corinthians'. *Holiness and Ecclesiology in the New Testament*. ed. Kent Brower and Andy Johnson (Grand Rapids: Eerdmans, 2007) 201–18.

——, 'Revisiting 1 Corinthians 11:27–34: Paul's Discussion of the Lord's Supper and African Meals' in *JSNT* 30 (2007), 95–112.

Banks, Robert, *Paul's Idea of Community* (Peabody: Hendrickson, 1994, 2nd edn).

Barclay, John M. G., *Obeying the Truth: A Study of Paul's Ethics in Galatians*, Studies of the New Testament and its World, ed. John Riches (Edinburgh: T&T Clark, 1988).

Barrett, C. K., *The Epistle to the Romans*, BNTC (London: A & C Black, 1962, 1971).

Beale, Greg K., 'The Eschatological Conception of New Testament Theology' in *'The Reader Must Understand': Eschatology in Bible and Theology*, ed. K. E. Brower and M. W. Elliott (Leicester: Apollos, IVP, 1997) 31–52.

Beker, J. C., *Paul's Apocalyptic Gospel*. Philadelphia: Fortress, 1985.

——, *Paul the Apostle: The Triumph of God in Life and Thought* (Philadelphia/Edinburgh: Fortress/T&T Clark, 1980).

——, *The Triumph of God* (Philadelphia: Fortress, 1990).

Best, Ernest, *The First and Second Epistles to the Thessalonians*. BNTC (London/Peabody: A & C Black/Hendrickson, 1972).

Blomberg, Craig L., *Contagious Holiness: Jesus' Meals with Sinners*. New Studies in Biblical Theology. ed. D. A. Carson (Leicester/Downers Grove: Apollos-IVP/IVP, 2005).

Bockmuehl, Markus, *A Commentary on the Epistle to the Philippians*, BNTC (London: A & C Black, 1997).

Borg, Marcus, *Conflict, Holiness and Politics in the Teachings of Jesus* (London: Continuum, 1998. Revised edn).

Braaten, Laurie J., 'All Creation Groans: Romans 8:22 in Light of the Biblical Sources'. *Horizons in Biblical Theology* 28 (2006), 131–59.

Brooke, George J., 'From Qumran to Corinth: Embroidered Allusions to Women's Authority'. *The Dead Sea Scrolls and the New Testament* (London/Philadelphia: SPCK/Fortress, 2005), 195–214.

Brower, K. E., 'Eschatology', *New Dictionary of Biblical Theology* (Leicester: IVP, 2000).

——, '1 Thessalonians'. Asbury Bible Commentary (Grand Rapids: Zondervan, 1992).

——, 'Jesus and the Lustful Eye: Glancing at Matthew 5:28'. *Evangelical Quarterly* 76 (2004), 291–309.

——, 'The Human Condition in Romans,' *European Explorations in Christian Holiness*, Vol. 2 (2001), 217–36.

——, *Holiness in the Gospels* (Kansas City: Beacon Hill, 2005).

——, 'The Holy One and his Disciples': Holiness and Ecclesiology in Mark', *Holiness and Ecclesiology in the New Testament*. ed. Kent Brower and Andy Johnson (Grand Rapids: Eerdmans, 2007), 57–75.

Brower, Kent E. and Andy Johnson, ed., *Holiness and Ecclesiology in the New Testament* (Grand Rapids: Eerdmans, 2007).

Bruce, F. F., *Paul: Apostle of the Free Spirit* (Exeter: Paternoster, 1977).

——, *1 and 2 Thessalonians*. WBC (Waco: Word, 1982).

Cadbury, Henry J., 'A Qumran Parallel to Paul'. *Harvard Theological Review* 51 (1958), 1–2.

Campbell, William S., *Paul and the Creation of Christian Identity*. Library of New Testament Studies 322 (London: T&T Clark, an imprint of Continuum, 2006).

Childs, B. S., *The Book of Exodus*. OTL (Philadelphia: Westminster, 1974).

Ciampa, Roy E. and Brian S. Rosner. 'The Structure and Argument of 1 Corinthians: A Biblical/Jewish Approach'. *NTS* 52 (2006), 205–18.

Cranfield, C. E. B., *A Critical and Exegetical Commentary on the Epistle to the Romans*. Vol. 1. ICC (Edinburgh: T&T Clark, 1975).

Davies, G. I., 'The Presence of God in the Second Temple and Rabbinic Doctrine'. *Templum Amicitiae*. ed. W. Horbury. *JSNTSS* 48 (Sheffield: JSOT, 1991).

Deasley, A. R. G., *The Shape of Qumran Theology*. The 1983 Didsbury Lectures (Carlisle: Paternoster, 2000).

Dodd, C. H., *Apostolic Preaching and its Developments* (Cambridge: Cambridge University Press, 1936).

Driver, J., *Understanding the Atonement for the Mission of the Church* (Scottdale: Herald, 1985).

Dumbrell, William J., *Covenant and Creation: A Theology of the Old Testament Covenants* (Exeter: Paternoster, 1984).

Dunham, John I., *Exodus*. WBC 3 (Waco: Word, 1987).

Dunn, James D. G., *The Epistle to the Galatians*. BNTC (Peabody: Hendrickson, 1993).

——, *1 Corinthians*. NTG (Sheffield: Sheffield Academic Press, 1995).

——, ' "The Law of Faith," "the Law of the Spirit" and "the Law of Christ" '. *Theology and Ethics in Paul and his Interpreters: Essays in Honor of Victor Paul Furnish*. ed. Eugene H. Lovering, Jr. and Jerry L. Sumney (Nashville: Abingdon, 1996) 62–82.

——, *Romans 1—8*. WBC (Waco: Word, 1988).

——, *Romans 9—15*. WBC (Waco: Word, 1988).

——, *The Theology of Paul the Apostle* (Edinburgh: T&T Clark, 1998).

——, *The Theology of Paul's Epistle to the Galatians*. NTT (Cambridge: Cambridge University Press, 1993).

Fach, Sandra E., 'Romans Five', unpublished paper presented to the MA seminar at Nazarene Theological College, 1996.

Fee, Gordon, *God's Empowering Presence: The Holy Spirit in the Letters of Paul* (Peabody: Hendrickson, 1994).

Fish, Bruce, 'Pseudo-Philo, Paul and Israel's Rolling Stone: Early Points along an Exegetical Trajectory'. *Israel in the Wilderness: Interpretations of the Biblical Narratives in the Jewish and Christian Traditions*. Themes in Biblical Narrative: Jewish and Christian Traditions 10. ed. Kenneth E. Pomykala (Leiden/Boston: Brill, 2008), 117–36.

Flemming, Dean, 'On Earth as It Is in Heaven': Holiness and the People of God in Revelation'. *Holiness and Ecclesiology in the New Testament*. ed. Kent Brower and Andy Johnson (Grand Rapids: Eerdmans, 2007), 343–62.

Fowl, Stephen, "Christology and Ethics in Paul," *Where Christology Began: Essays on Philippians 2*. ed. Ralph P. Martin and Brian J. Dodd (Louisville: Westminster John Knox, 1998), 140–53.

——, *The Story of Christ in the Ethics of Paul*. JSNTSS 36 (Sheffield: JSOT Press, 1990).

France, R. T., *Women in Ministry: A test case for biblical interpretation*. The 1995 Didsbury Lectures (Carlisle: Paternoster, 1997).

Garlington, Don B., *'The Obedience of Faith': A Pauline Phrase in Historical Context*. WUNT 2, Reihe 38 (Tübingen: J. C. B. Mohr (Paul Siebeck). 1991).

Gaventa, Beverley Roberts, 'The Cosmic Power of Sin in Paul's Letter to the Romans'. *Interpretation* 58 (2004), 229–40.

Gorman, Michael J., *Apostle of the Crucified Lord* (Grand Rapids: Eerdmans, 2005).

——, *Cruciformity: Paul's Narrative Spirituality of the Cross* (Grand Rapids: Eerdmans, 2001).

——, ' "You Shall be Cruciform for I am Cruciform": Paul's Trinitarian Reconstruction of Holiness'. *Holiness and Ecclesiology in the New Testament*. ed. Kent Brower and Andy Johnson (Grand Rapids: Eerdmans, 2007, 148–66).

Greathouse, William M., 'A Pauline Theology of Sanctification'. Ed. H. Ray Dunning and Neil B. Wiseman. *Biblical Resources for Holiness Preaching*. Vol. 1 (Kansas City: Beacon Hill, 1990), 29–50.

——, *Romans 1—8: A Commentary in the Wesleyan Tradition*. New Beacon Bible Commentary (Kansas City: Beacon Hill, 2008).

——, *Romans 9—16: A Commentary in the Wesleyan Tradition*, New Beacon Bible Commentary (Kansas City: Beacon Hill, 2008).

——, *Wholeness in Christ: Toward a Biblical Theology of Holiness* (Kansas City: Beacon Hill, 1998).

Grieb, A. Katherine, *The Story of Romans: A Narrative Defense of God's Righteousness* (Louisville/London: Westminster John Knox, 2002).

Gundry, Robert H., *Soma in Biblical Theology, with Emphasis on Pauline Anthropology*. SNTSMS 29 (Cambridge: Cambridge University Press, 1975).

Gunton, Colin E., *Christ and Creation*. 1990 Didsbury Lectures (Carlisle, Paternoster, 1993).

Hafemann, Scot J., 'The Covenant Relationship'. *Central Themes in Biblical Theology: Mapping Unity in Diversity*. ed. Scott F. Hafemann and Paul R. House (Nottingham: IVP, 2007).

Harrington, Hannah, *Holiness: Rabbinic Judaism and the Graeco-Roman World* (London/New York: Routledge, 2001).

Hauerwas, Stanley, *Sanctify them in the Truth: Holiness Exemplified* (Edinburgh/Nashville: T&T Clark/Abingdon, 1998).

Hayes, Christine E., *Gentile Impurities and Jewish Identities: Intermarriage and Conversion from the Bible to the Talmud* (Oxford: Oxford University Press, 2002).

Hays, Richard B., 'Christ Died for the Ungodly: Narrative Soteriology in Paul?' Unpublished paper for the Society of Biblical Literature Pauline Soteriology Ground, Atlanta, 24 November 2003.

——, *Echoes of Scripture in the Letters of Paul* (New Haven: Yale, 1989).

——, *First Corinthians*. Interpretation (Louisville: John Knox, 1997).

——, 'The Role of Scripture in Paul's Ethics' in *Theology and Ethics in Paul and his Interpreters: Essays in Honor of Victor Paul Furnish*. ed. Eugene H. Lovering, Jr. and Jerry L. Sumney (Nashville: Abingdon, 1996), 30–47.

Heil, John P., *Ephesians: Empowerment to Walk in Love for the Unity of All in Christ*, Studies in Biblical Literature 13 (Atlanta: Society of Biblical Literature, 2007).

Hooker, Morna D., 'Adam in Romans 1', *From Adam to Christ: Essays on Paul* (Cambridge: Cambridge University Press, 1990).

——, 'A Partner in the Gospel: Paul's Understanding of his Ministry'. *Theology and Ethics in Paul and his Interpreters: Essays in Honor of Victor Paul Furnish*. ed. by Eugene Lovering, Jr. and Jerry L Sumney (Nashville: Abingdon, 1996), 83–100.

——, 'ΠΙΣΤΟΣ ΞΡΙΣΤΟΥ', *NTS* 35 (1989), 321–42.

Horrell, David G., *The Social Ethos of the Corinthian Correspondence* (Edinburgh: T&T Clark, 1996).

Horrell, David, Cherryl Hunt, Christopher Southgate, 'Appeals to the Bible in Ecotheology and Environmental Ethics: a Typology of Hermeneutical Stances'. *Studies in Christian Ethics* 21 (2008), 219–38.

Hubbard, Moyer V., *New Creation in Paul's Letters and Thought*. SNTSMS 119 (Cambridge: Cambridge University Press, 2002).

Hurtado, L. W., *At the Origins of Christian Worship*. The 2000 Didsbury Lectures (Carlisle: Paternoster, 2000).

——, 'Jesus as Lordly Example in Philippians 2:5–11'. *From Jesus to Paul: Studies in Honour of Francis Wright Beare*. ed. P. Richardson and J. Hurd (Waterloo: Wilfrid Laurier University Press, 1984), 113–26.

Jervis, L. Ann, 'Becoming like God through Christ: Discipleship in Romans' in *Patterns of Discipleship in the New Testament*. ed. Richard N. Longenecker. McMaster New Testament Studies (Grand Rapids: Eerdmans, 1996).

Jewett, Robert, *Romans: A Commentary*, Hermeneia: A Critical and Historical Commentary on the Bible (Minneapolis: Fortress, an imprint of Augsburg Fortress, 2007).

Johnson, Andy, 'The Sanctification of the Imagination in 1 Thessalonians'. *Holiness and Ecclesiology in the New Testament.* ed. Kent Brower and Andy Johnson (Grand Rapids: Eerdmans, 2007), 275–92.

Käsemann, E., *Commentary on Romans.* Translated by Geoffrey W. Bromiley (Grand Rapids: Eerdmans, 1980).

Klawans, Jonathan, *Impurity and Sin in Ancient Judaism* (Oxford: Oxford University Press, 2000).

Leclerc, Diane, 'Holiness and Power: Toward a Wesleyan Theology of Dis-Ability'. *Wesleyan Theological Journal* 44 (2009), 55–69.

Lincoln, Andrew T., 'From Wrath to Justification: Tradition, Gospel, and Audience in the Theology of Romans 1:18 – 4:25'. *Pauline Theology, Vol. III Romans.* ed. David M. Hay and E. Elizabeth Johnson (Minneapolis: Fortress Augsburg, 1994).

Longenecker, Richard N., 'The Focus of Romans' in *Romans and the People of God.* FS for Gordon D. Fee. ed. Sven K. Soderland and N. T. Wright (Grand Rapids/Cambridge: Eerdmans, 1999).

Macdonald, Margaret Y., 'Slavery, Sexuality and House Churches: A Reassessment of Colossians 3:18—4:1 in Light of New Research on the Roman Family'. *NTS* 53 (2007), 94–113.

Marshall, I Howard, *1 and 2 Thessalonians.* NCB (Grand Rapids: Eerdmans, 1983).

Martens, Elmer A., 'People of God'. *Central Themes in Biblical Theology: Mapping Unity in Diversity.* ed. Scott F. Hafemann and Paul R. House (Nottingham: IVP, 2007), 225–53.

Martin, Dale, *The Corinthian Body.* New Haven: Yale, 1995.

Martyn, J. Louis. *Galatians.* AB 33A (New York/London: Doubleday, 1997).

May, Alistair Scott, *'The Body for the Lord': Sex and Identity in 1 Corinthians 5—7,* JSNTSS 278 (London: T&T Clark International, an imprint of Continuum, 2004).

Mentch, Donald P., 'Righteousness, Peace and Joy in the Holy Spirit: Holiness and Ethics in Paul's Epistle to the Romans'. MA dissertation, Nazarene Theological College, 1998.

Moo, Douglas, *The Epistle to the Romans.* NICNT (Grand Rapids: Eerdmans, 1996).

Moo, Jonathan, 'Romans 8:19–22 and Isaiah's Cosmic Covenant'. *NTS* 54 (2008), 74–89.

Mullen, J. Patrick, *Dining with Pharisees* (Collegeville: Liturgical, 2004).

Munzinger, André, *Discerning the Spirits: Theological and Ethical Hermeneutics in Paul.* SNTSMS 140 (Cambridge: Cambridge University Press, 2007).

Newton, Michael, *The Concept of Purity at Qumran and in the Letters of Paul*. SNTSMS 53 (Cambridge: Cambridge University Press, 1985).

Njiru, Paul Kariuki, *Charisms and the Holy Spirit's Activity in the Body of Christ: An Exegetical-Theological Study of 1 Corinthians 12, 4–11 and Romans 12, 6–8*. Tesi Gregoriana: Serie Teologia 86 (Roma: Editrice Pontificia Universita Gregoriana, 2002).

Nwachukwu, Maru Sylvia, *Creation-Covenant Scheme and Justification by Faith: A Canonical Study of the God-Human Drama in the Pentateuch and the Letter to the Romans*, Tesi Gregoriana: Serie Teologia 89 (Roma: Editrice Pontificia Universita Gregoriana, 2002).

Oakes, Peter, *Philippians: From People to Letter*, SNTSMS 110 (Cambridge: Cambridge University Press, 2001).

——, 'Made Holy by the Holy Spirit: Holiness and Ecclesiology in Romans'. *Holiness and Ecclesiology in the New Testament*. ed. Kent Brower and Andy Johnson (Grand Rapids: Eerdmans, 2007), 167–86.

Packer, J. I., 'The "Wretched Man" Revisited: Another Look at Romans 7:14–25'. *Romans and the People of God*. FS for Gordon D Fee. ed. Sven K. Soderlund and N. T. Wright (Grand Rapids/Cambridge: Eerdmans/Cambridge University Press, 1999), 70–81.

Peterson, David G., *Possessed by God: A New Testament Theology of Sanctification and Holiness*. New Studies in Biblical Theology (Leicester: Apollos/IVP, 1995).

Piper, John, *The Future of Justification: A Response to N. T. Wright* (Nottingham; IVP, 2008).

Poirier, John C., 'Purity beyond the Temple in the Second Temple Era'. *JBL* 122 (2003), 247–65.

Rapinchuk, Mark, 'Universal Sin and Salvation in Romans 5:12–21', a paper read at the Fiftieth National Conference of the Evangelical Theological Society. 1998. Published on microfiche as part of *Evangelical Theological Society Papers*. ETS–5018, 1999.

Rapske, Brian, *The Book of Acts and Paul in Roman Custody*. The Book of Acts in its First Century Setting. Vol. 3 (Grand Rapids: Eerdmans, 1994).

Robinson, J. A. T., *The Body: A study in Pauline Theology*. SBT 5 (London: SCM, 1952).

Rosner, Brian S., *Paul's Scripture and Ethics: A Study of I Corinthians 5–7*. Arbeiten Zur Geschichte Des Antiken Judentums und Des Urchristentums (Tûbingen: J. C. B. Mohr, 1994).

Sampley, J. Paul, *The First Letter to the Corinthians*. NIB. Vol. X (Nashville: Abingdon, 2002).

Sanders, E. P., *Paul,* Past Masters (Oxford: Oxford University Press, 1991).

Schreiner, Thomas R., *Paul, Apostle of God's Glory in Christ* (Downer's Grove: IVP, 2001).

——, 'The Commands of God'. *Central Themes in Biblical Theology: Mapping Unity in Diversity.* ed. Scott F. Hafemann and Paul R. House (Nottingham: IVP, 2007), 66–101.

——, *Romans.* Baker Exegetical Commentary on the New Testament (Grand Rapids: Baker, 1998).

Seifrid, Mark, 'Righteousness Language in the Hebrew Scriptures and Early Judaism' in *Justification and Variegated Nomism. Vol. 1—The Complexities of Second Temple Judaism.* ed. by D. A. Carson, Peter T. O'Brien and Mark A. Seifrid (Tübingen: J. C. B. Mohr [Paul Siebeck], 2001).

Sherwin-White, A. N., *Roman Citizenship* (Oxford: Oxford University Press, 1973).

Snodgrass, Klyne. 'The Gospel in Romans: A Theology of Revelation'. *The Gospel in Paul: Studies on Corinthians, Galatians and Romans.* FS for Richard N Longenecker. ed. by L. Ann Jervis and Peter Richardson. JSNTSS 108 (Sheffield: Sheffield Academic Press, 1994).

Stubbs, David L., 'The Shape of Soteriology and the *Pistos Christou* Debate' in *SJT* 61 (2008), 137–57.

Stuhlmacher, Peter, *Paul's Letter to the Romans: A Commentary.* Translated by Scott F. Hafemann (Louisville: Westminster/John Knox, 1994).

Swartley, Willard, *Slavery, Sabbath, War and Women: Case Issues in Biblical Interpretation* (Scottsdale: Herald Press, 1987).

Taylor, Vincent, *Jesus and His Sacrifice: a Study of the Passion Sayings of the Gospels* (London: Macmillan, 1937).

Thielman, Frank, 'The Story of Israel and the Theology of Romans 5 – 8,' in *Pauline Theology, Vol III. Romans.* ed. David M. Hay and E. Elizabeth Johnson (Minneapolis: Fortress Augsburg, 1994).

Thiselton, A C., *The First Epistle to the Corinthians,* The New International Greek Testament Commentary (Carlisle: Paternoster, 2000).

du Toit, Andrie B., 'Forensic Metaphors in Romans and their Soteriological Significance'. *Salvation in the New Testament: Perspectives on Soteriology.* ed. by Jan G. van der Watt. NovTS. 121 (Leiden: Brill, 2005), 213–46.

Wagner, J. Ross, 'Working Out Salvation: Holiness and Community in Philippians'. *Holiness and Ecclesiology in the New Testament.* ed.

Kent Brower and Andy Johnson (Grand Rapids: Eerdmans, 2007), 257–74.

Walsh, Brian J. and Sylvia C. Keesmaat, *Colossians Remixed: Subverting the Empire* (Carlisle: Paternoster, 2004).

Wanamaker, C. A., *Commentary on 1 & 2 Thessalonians*. NIGNTC (Grand Rapids/Exeter: Eerdmans/Paternoster, 1990).

Ware, T., *The Orthodox Church* (Harmondsworth: Penguin, 1993. Revised edn).

Watson, Francis, *Agape, Eros, Gender: towards a Pauline sexual ethics* (Cambridge: Cambridge University Press), 2000.

——, 'The Authority of the Voice: A Theological Reading of 1 Cor. 11:2—16'. *NTS* 46 (2000), 520–36.

Wedderburn, A. J. M., *The Reasons for Romans*. SNTW (Edinburgh: T&T Clark, 1988).

Weima, Jeffrey A. D., ' "How you must walk to please God": Holiness and Discipleship in 1 Thessalonians'. *Patterns of Discipleship in the New Testament*. ed. Richard N. Longenecker. McMaster New Testament Studies (Grand Rapids: Eerdmans, 1996), 98–121.

Wenham, David, *Paul: Follower of Jesus or Founder of Christianity?* (Grand Rapids: Eerdmans, 1995).

Whittle, Sarah, '2 Corinthians 6:14 – 7:1. "Come Out From Among Them!" Calling the Corinthians to Covenant Holiness'. MA thesis, University of Manchester, 2007.

Williamson, Paul R., *Sealed with an Oath: Covenant in God's Unfolding Purpose*. New Studies in Biblical Theology 23 (Leicester: Apollos/IVP, 2007).

Winter, Bruce, *Seek the Welfare of the City: Christians as Benefactors and Citizens* (Grand Rapids: Eerdmans, 1994).

——, 'Carnal Conduct and Sanctification in 1 Corinthians: *simul sanctus et peccator?*' *Holiness and Ecclesiology in the New Testament*. ed. Kent Brower and Andy Johnson (Grand Rapids: Eerdmans, 2007), 184–200.

Witherington III, Ben. *Conflict and Community in Corinth* (Carlisle: Paternoster, 1995).

——, *Paul's Narrative Thought World: The Tapestry of Tragedy and Triumph* (Louisville: John Knox/Westminster, 1994).

Wright, N. T., *The Climax of the Covenant: Christ and the Law in Pauline Theology* (Edinburgh: T&T Clark, 1991).

——, *The Epistle of Paul to the Romans*. NIB. Vol X (Nashville: Abingdon, 2002).

——, 'New Exodus, New Inheritance: the Narrative Substructure of Romans 3—8,' in *Romans and the People of God*, FS for Gordon D. Fee. ed. Sven K. Soderland and N. T. Wright (Grand Rapids/Cambridge: Eerdmans, 1999).

——, 'New Perspective on Paul', unpublished paper delivered to the 10th Edinburgh Dogmatics Conference, Rutherford House, Edinburgh, 25–28 August 2003.

——, *The New Testament and the People of God*, volume one of *Christian Origins and the Question of God* (London: SPCK, 1992).

——, 'Romans and the Theology of Paul,' *Pauline Theology, Vol. III Romans*. ed. David M. Hay and E. Elizabeth Johnson (Minneapolis: Fortress Augsburg, 1994).

Yates, John W., *The Spirit and Creation in Paul*. WUNT 2, Reiche 251 (Iwlingen Mohr Siebech, 2008).

Ziesler, J. A., *The Epistle to the Galatians* (London: Epworth, 1992).

——, *The Meaning of Righteousness in Paul: A Linguistic and Theological Enquiry*, SNTSMS 20 (Cambridge: Cambridge University Press, 1972).

——, *Pauline Christianity*, The Oxford Bible Series, revised edition (Oxford: Oxford University Press, 1990).

——, *Romans*, Trinity Press International New Testament Commentaries (London/Philadelphia: SCM/TPI, 1989).

Notes

Chapter One: Paul and Holiness

1 Except for instances where the translations are my own, all translations are taken from the New Revised Standard Version.

2 See, for example, Marcus Borg, *Conflict, Holiness and Politics in the Teachings of Jesus* (London: Continuum, 1998, revised edition); N. T. Wright, *The New Testament and the People of God,* volume one of Christian Origins and the Question of God (London: SPCK, 1992). For a short summary of the context of holiness in the late second temple period see K. E. Brower, *Holiness in the Gospels* (Kansas City: Beacon Hill, 2005).

3 See Jonathan Klawans, *Impurity and Sin in Ancient Judaism* (Oxford: Oxford University Press, 2000), 138.

4 John C. Poirier, in 'Purity beyond the Temple in the Second Temple Era', *JBL* 122 (2003), 249, points to a wider concern with purity than simply with the temple.

5 See J. Patrick Mullen, *Dining with Pharisees* (Collegeville: Liturgical, 2004) and Craig L. Blomberg, *Contagious Holiness: Jesus' Meals with Sinners,* New Studies in Biblical Theology, ed. D. A. Carson (Leicester/Downers Grove: Apollos-IVP/IVP, 2005).

6 Thomas R. Schreiner, 'The Commands of God' in *Central Themes in Biblical Theology: Mapping Unity in Diversity,* ed. Scott F. Hafemann and Paul R. House (Nottingham: IVP, 2007), 66–101 (85).

7 The polemic in Matthew 23 may owe as much to the struggle for the soul of Judaism between followers of Jesus and the Pharisees as it does to the hypocritical character of Pharisaism per se.

8 See Michael Newton, *The Concept of Purity at Qumran and in the Letters of Paul*, SNTSMS 53 (Cambridge: Cambridge University Press, 1985) and A. R. G. Deasley, *The Shape of Qumran Theology*, The 1983 Didsbury Lectures (Carlisle: Paternoster, 2000).

9 Schreiner, 'Commands', 95.

10 See Scott J. Hafemann, 'The Covenant Relationship' in *Central Themes in Biblical Theology: Mapping Unity in Diversity*, ed. Scott F. Hafemann and Paul R. House (Nottingham: IVP, 2007), 20–65 who states 'God's grace and calling do not enable obedience. Rather, they bring it about' (64; see also 54).

11 See J. A. Ziesler, *Pauline Christianity*, The Oxford Bible Series, revised edition (Oxford: Oxford University Press, 1990), 69.

12 See, for example, William S. Campbell, *Paul and the Creation of Christian Identity*, Library of New Testament Studies 322 (London: T&T Clark, an imprint of Continuum, 2006).

13 Hafemann, 'Covenant', 30. See also 49–56.

14 Klawans, *Impurity and Sin in Ancient Judaism*, 151.

15 Elmer A. Martens, 'People of God' in *Central Themes in Biblical Theology: Mapping Unity in Diversity*, ed. Scott F. Hafemann and Paul R. House (Nottingham: IVP, 2007): 225–53 (244).

16 Michael J. Gorman, ' "You Shall be Cruciform for I am Cruciform": Paul's Trinitarian Reconstruction of Holiness', in *Holiness and Ecclesiology in the New Testament*, ed. Kent Brower and Andy Johnson (Grand Rapids: Eerdmans, 2007), 148–66 (148), hereafter *HENT*.

17 See J. C. Beker, *Paul the Apostle: The Triumph of God in Life and Thought* (Philadelphia/Edinburgh: Fortress/T&T Clark, 1980) who makes this coherence-contingency axis the major interpretative grid for understanding Paul. Paul may well assume that his readers know more than they actually do.

18 David L. Stubbs, 'The Shape of Soteriology and the *Pistos Christou* Debate' in *SJT* 61 (2008), 137–57 (139).

19 N. T. Wright, 'Romans and the Theology of Paul,' in *Pauline Theology, Vol III Romans*, ed. David M. Hay and E. Elizabeth Johnson (Minneapolis: Fortress Augsburg, 1994), 34, italics original.

20 See, for example, E. Käsemann, *Commentary on Romans*, trans. Geoffrey W. Bromiley (Grand Rapids: Eerdmans, 1980) and Beker, *Paul*.

21 J. C. Beker, *The Triumph of God* (Philadelphia: Fortress, 1990);
    J. A. Ziesler, *Pauline Christianity*, revised edition (Oxford: Oxford
    University Press, 1990).

22 See N. T. Wright, 'New Perspective on Paul', (paper delivered to
    the 10th Edinburgh Dogmatics Conference, Rutherford House,
    Edinburgh, 25–28 August 2003). See also, for example, the work
    of Richard B. Hays, *Echoes of Scripture in the Letters of Paul* (New
    Haven: Yale, 1989), N. T. Wright, *The Climax of the Covenant:
    Christ and the Law in Pauline Theology* (Edinburgh: T&T Clark,
    1991) and J. D. G. Dunn, *The Theology of Paul the Apostle* (Edinburgh:
    T&T Clark, 1998).

23 See A. J. M. Wedderburn, *The Reasons for Romans*, SNTW (Edin-
    burgh: T&T Clark, 1988). See especially Campbell, *Identity*.

24 See L. W. Hurtado, *At the Origins of Christian Worship*, The 2000
    Didsbury Lectures (Carlisle: Paternoster, 2000).

25 Wright, 'Romans', 33.

26 See Peter Oakes, 'Made Holy by the Holy Spirit: Holiness and
    Ecclesiology in Romans,' in *HENT*: 167–86.

27 The extent to which it is the central datum of Paul's theology
    is disputed. See Thomas R. Schreiner, *Paul, Apostle of God's Glory
    in Christ* (Downer's Grove: IVP, 2001), 196–209, who argues
    for its importance, although not exclusive centrality, while
    reasserting, albeit in slightly nuanced form, the traditional
    Lutheran and forensic understanding.

28 Andrie B. du Toit, 'Forensic Metaphors in Romans and their
    Soteriological Significance' in *Salvation in the New Testament:
    Perspectives on Soteriology*, ed. Jan G. van der Watt, NovTS 121
    (Leiden: Brill, 2005), 213–46.

29 Du Toit, 'Forensic Metaphors', 243.

30 For a robust response to Wright's views from a trenchant
    Reformed perspective, see John Piper, *The Future of Justification:
    A Response to N. T. Wright* (Nottingham: IVP, 2008).

31 J. A. Ziesler, *The Meaning of Righteousness in Paul: A Linguistic
    and Theological Enquiry*, SNTSMS 20 (Cambridge: Cambridge
    University Press, 1972).

32 Ziesler, *Righteousness*, 1.

33 Ziesler, *Righteousness*, 20. But see the criticism of this view in
    Mark Seifrid, 'Righteousness Language in the Hebrew Scrip-
    tures and Early Judaism' in *Justification and Variegated Nomism.
    Vol 1—The Complexities of Second Temple Judaism*, ed. D. A. Carson,

Peter T. O'Brien and Mark A. Seifrid (Tübingen: J. C. B. Mohr [Paul Siebeck], 2001), 415–42.

34 A. Katherine Grieb, *The Story of Romans: A Narrative Defense of God's Righteousness* (Louisville/London: Westminster John Knox, 2002), 13.

35 *Sedeqah* is a relational concept in the OT, primarily designating covenant faithfulness.

36 Wright, 'Romans', 33, emphasis original.

37 See Seifrid, 'Righteousness Language'.

38 See especially William J. Dumbrell, *Covenant and Creation: A Theology of the Old Testament Covenants* (Exeter: Paternoster, 1984), critiqued in Paul R. Williamson, *Sealed with an Oath: Covenant in God's Unfolding Purpose*, New Studies in Biblical Theology 23 (Leicester: Apollos/IVP, 2007), 69–76. Williamson, *Oath*, 75.

39 Williamson, *Oath*, 75.

40 Williamson, *Oath*, 76.

41 Maru Sylvia Nwachukwu, *Creation-Covenant Scheme and Justification by Faith: A Canonical Study of the God-Human Drama in the Pentateuch and the Letter to the Romans*, Tesi Gregoriana: Serie Teologia 89 (Roma: Editrice Pontificia Universita Gregoriana, 2002), 250.

42 Seifrid, 'Righteousness Language', 426.

43 Nwachukwu, *Creation-Covenant Scheme*, 137.

44 Andrew T. Lincoln, 'From Wrath to Justification: Tradition, Gospel, and Audience in the Theology of Romans 1:18—4:25,' in *Pauline Theology, Vol III Romans*, ed. David M. Hay and E. Elizabeth Johnson (Minneapolis: Fortress Augsburg, 1994), 148.

45 See Peter Stuhlmacher, *Paul's Letter to the Romans: A Commentary*, trans. Scott F. Hafemann (Louisville: Westminster/John Knox, 1994 ET), 82.

46 Klyne Snodgrass, 'The Gospel in Romans: A Theology of Revelation', in *The Gospel in Paul: Studies on Corinthians, Galatians and Romans*, FS for Richard N. Longenecker, ed. L. Ann Jervis and Peter Richardson, JSNTSS 108 (Sheffield: SAP, 1994), 314. The argument he makes is that 'justification is not the category under which revelation is subsumed, but rather justification is subsumed under and comprehended from the category of revelation. Now the debate about whether justification is to be

understood as "declarative" or "effective" (a making righteous) is nuanced differently, for focus on the revelation of God means that God is met in the gospel, not merely that God says something. One is not merely declared righteous; rather one is transformed by encounter with the powerful God who places people in right relation to himself.'

47 See J. Driver, *Understanding the Atonement for the Mission of the Church* (Scottdale: Herald, 1985), 204.

48 See the excellent article by Morna D. Hooker, 'ΠΙΣΤΟΣ ΧΡΙΣΤΟΥ', in *NTS* 35 (1989), 321–42.

49 Wright, *Climax*, 38–40.

50 Wright, *Climax*, 38–40.

51 Wright, 'New Perspective', no page.

52 Wright, 'Romans,' 34, emphasis original.

53 Wright, *Romans*, 578–79, italics original.

54 Wright, *Romans*, 578.

55 E. P. Sanders, *Paul*, Past Masters (Oxford: Oxford University Press, 1991), 48. See also Ziesler, *Pauline*.

56 J. A. Ziesler, *Romans*, Trinity Press International New Testament Commentaries (London/Philadelphia: SCM/TPI, 1989), 71.

57 See N. T. Wright, 'New Exodus, New Inheritance: the Narrative Substructure of Romans 3—8,' in *Romans and the People of God*, FS for Gordon D. Fee, ed. Sven K. Soderland and N. T. Wright (Grand Rapids/Cambridge: Eerdmans, 1999), 26–36 (33).

58 Richard B. Hays, 'The Role of Scripture in Paul's Ethics', in *Theology and Ethics in Paul and his Interpreters: Essays in Honor of Victor Paul Furnish*, ed. Eugene H. Lovering, Jr. and Jerry L. Sumney (Nashville: Abingdon, 1996), 30–47 (34).

59 Stuhlmacher, *Romans*, 64.

60 See Dunn, *Romans 1—8*, WBC (Waco: Word, 1988), 40f. and *Theology*, 340–46.

61 See Wright, 'New Exodus', 33.

62 Schreiner, *Paul*, 209.

63 Schreiner, *Paul*, 209.

64 Nwachukwu, *Creation-Covenant Scheme*, 286.

65 This section is a revised and shorter version of K. E. Brower, 'The Human Condition in Romans,' in *European Explorations in Christian Holiness*, Vol 2 (2001), 217–36. Used with permission.

66 But see Richard N. Longenecker, 'The Focus of Romans: The Central Role of 5:1—8:39 in the Argument of the Letter' in *Romans and the People of God*, 49–69 (63).

67 See Lincoln, 'From Wrath to Justification', 138.

68 Morna D. Hooker, 'Adam in Romans 1', *From Adam to Christ: Essays on Paul* (Cambridge: Cambridge University Press, 1990), 83.

69 See Stanley Hauerwas, *Sanctify them in the Truth: Holiness Exemplified* (Edinburgh/Nashville: T&T Clark/Abingdon, 1998), 253, 'while creation encompasses nature, when you say nature you have not said creation.'

70 Nwachukwu, *Creation-Covenant Scheme*, 251.

71 An important point – Paul does not have an independent or personified view of nature.

72 Frank Thielman, 'The Story of Israel and the Theology of Romans 5—8,' in *Pauline Theology, Vol III Romans*, 149, notes that 'The fundamental point of Paul's discussion in 5:12–21, then, is that Christ is God's answer to the disasters created by Adam's sin and Israel's violation of the covenant' (181).

73 For full details and analysis of the various options here, see C. E. B. Cranfield, *A Critical and Exegetical Commentary on the Epistle to the Romans*, Vol 1, ICC (Edinburgh: T&T Clark, 1975), 272 n. 5, and Douglas Moo, *The Epistle to the Romans*, NICNT (Grand Rapids: Eerdmans, 1996), 318 n. 19.

74 See C. K. Barrett, *The Epistle to the Romans*, BNTC (London: A & C Black, 1962, 1971), 111.

75 Moo, *Romans*, 323.

76 See Mark Rapinchuk, 'Universal Sin and Salvation in Romans 5:12–21' (paper read at the Fiftieth National Conference of the Evangelical Theological Society [1998] and published on microfiche as part of *Evangelical Theological Society Papers* [ETS – 5018, 1999]), 7. Even in the much-cited statement in Romans 3:9b, Paul's primarily thinks of groups: *we have already charged that all, both Jews and Greeks, are under the power of sin.* The catena of six OT texts Paul cites (3:10–18) supports this view. All five Psalm citations contrast the wicked who are not God's people (i.e. Gentiles) with the righteous (i.e. Israel). But the final citation from Isaiah refers directly to the people of Israel, thus confirming Paul's point that Jews as well as Greeks, are under the power of sin. Paul is not here speaking of individuals.

77 Wright, *Climax*, 37.

78 Thielman, 'The Story of Israel', 195.

79 See now Beverley Roberts Gaventa, 'The Cosmic Power of Sin in Paul's Letter to the Romans' in *Interpretation* 58 (2004), 229–40 (235).

80 Gaventa, 'Cosmic Power', 236.

81 Ziesler, *Pauline Christianity*, 76.

82 The phrase 'sin that dwells in me' has been translated tendentiously in the NIV as 'sinful nature', giving an unfortunate reified connotation to indwelling sin.

83 Moo, *Romans*, 451.

84 The discussion is far more complex than these brief notes imply. A full discussion would have to consider the whole reason for writing Romans in general and the specific Jew–Gentile discussion in particular.

85 Thomas R. Schreiner, *Romans,* Baker Exegetical Commentary on the New Testament (Grand Rapids: Baker, 1998), 403.

86 Cranfield, *Romans*, 383 n. 2, suggests that 'Christ's life before his actual ministry and death was not just a standing where unfallen Adam had stood without yielding to the temptation to which Adam succumbed, but a matter of starting from where we start, subject to all the evil pressures which we inherit, and using the altogether unpromising and unsuitable material of our corrupt nature to work out a perfect, sinless obedience.'

87 William M. Greathouse, *Romans 1—8: A Commentary in the Wesleyan Tradition.* NBBC (Kansas City: Beacon Hill, 2008), 207.

88 Greathouse, *Romans 1—8*, 208.

89 The most important of these is Dunn, in several publications, most recently in *Theology*, 472–77. See the full and helpful discussion in Moo, *Romans*, 421–31. Some in the holiness movement have seen this chapter as referring to the experience of the not yet entirely sanctified. But William M. Greathouse, *Wholeness in Christ: Toward a Biblical Theology of Holiness* (Kansas City: Beacon Hill, 1998), 106, argues that it 'cannot be construed as depicting *Christian* experience'.

90 Moo, *Romans*, 444. J. I. Packer is a case in point. See 'The "Wretched Man" Revisited: Another Look at Romans 7:14–25', in *Romans and the People of God*: 70–81. Cranfield, *Romans*, 356, sees this as describing 'two different aspects, two contemporaneous realities, of the Christian life, both of which continue so

long as the Christian is in the flesh.' Dunn, *Theology*, 476, thinks that the view which takes 7:5 as a statement of fact 'simply promotes an idealistic and unrealistic perspective, for which postbaptismal sin is impossible in theory and theologically and pastorally disastrous in practice.'

91 Although he is not always consistent, in general Paul makes a distinction between 'body' (*sōma*) and 'flesh' (*sarx*). Generally, according to Dunn, *Theology*, 72, ' "body" denotes *a being in the world*' whereas "flesh" denotes *a belonging to the world* ... In broader terms, we could say that Paul's distinction between *soma* and *sarx* made possible a positive affirmation of human createdness and creation and of the interdependence of humanity within its created environment.'

92 According to Beker, *Paul*, 288, cited by Moo, *Romans*, 491 n. 104, the 'mortal body' is to be distinguished from the body of sin that is crucified with Christ (6:6).

93 Stuhlmacher, *Romans*, 116.

94 As Cranfield, *Romans*, 387 points out, Paul's use of the term 'flesh' here is not quite the same as in Galatians 2:20. In Galatians, Paul is speaking of the continued existence of the Christian in this present life, not the mindset of the Christian. Paul warns against the 'desires of the flesh' in Galatians 5:16.

95 See now John W. Yates, *The Spirit and Creation in Paul*, WUNT 2. 251 (Tübingen: Mohr, Siebeck, 2008), whose excellent discussion on the life-giving work of the spirit appeared too late for consideration in this book.

96 Had Paul been a modern writer, he may well have put inverted commas around 'slaves of righteousness' in light of what he states in Romans 8:15–17.

97 The MS evidence for the well-known textual variant between *echomen* and *echōmen* is not decisive. With Nestle's 27th, I read 'we have' because it fits better with Paul's theological narrative.

98 A quick look at the whole Pauline corpus shows well over forty uses of the term.

99 See Thielman, 'The Story of Israel', 181, who writes, 'The fundamental point of Paul's discussion in 5:12–21 is that Christ is God's answer to the disasters created by Adam's sin and Israel's violation of the covenant.'

100 See the summary and very helpful analysis of the big picture in Wright, *Climax*, 35–40.

101 Sandra Fach, 'Romans Five' (essay, Nazarene Theological College, 1996).
102 See Michael J. Gorman, *Cruciformity: Paul's Narrative Spirituality of the Cross* (Grand Rapids: Eerdmans, 2001). The word has now become common currency.
103 More will be said on this in Chapter 4.
104 The NIV translation here emphasises the love that has been given us; the NRSV notes the Holy Spirit. Paul speaks of the love of God far less than John does. But his statement in Romans 5 is decisive for understanding the reason for God's action. Paul would have agreed with John's incipient Trinitarian notion about the love that energises the Holy Trinity. Love can never be inward looking and so Paul here notes that *God proves his love for us in that while we still were sinners Christ died for us* (5:8).
105 Greathouse, *Romans 1—8*, 182.
106 Ziesler, *Romans*, 170.
107 Greathouse, *Romans 1—8*, 187.

Chapter Two: Holiness and the Holy Spirit

1 Gorman, 'Cruciform', 154, italics original.
2 Nwachukwu, *Creation-Covenant Scheme*, 288.
3 See Moo, *Romans*, 304 n. 51.
4 Wright, *Romans*, 517.
5 Gorman, 'Cruciform', 153, his italics.
6 See Peter Oakes, 'Romans', 180.
7 Gordon Fee, *God's Empowering Presence: The Holy Spirit in the Epistles of Paul* (Peabody: Hendrickson, 1994), 476.
8 Nwachukwu, *Creation-Covenant Scheme*, 288.
9 Oakes, 'Romans', 171.
10 Don B. Garlington, *'The Obedience of Faith': A Pauline Phrase in Historical Context*, WUNT 2, Reihe 38 (Tübingen: J. C. B. Mohr (Paul Siebeck), 1991), 254.
11 Oakes, 'Romans', 177.
12 Oakes, 'Romans', 178.
13 Gorman, 'Cruciform', 153.
14 Oakes, 'Romans', 173.

15 See C. H. Dodd, *Apostolic Preaching and its Developments* (Cambridge: Cambridge University Press, 1936). Similarly, Paul does not use the same mutual indwelling language as John does. See Brower, *Holiness in the Gospels.*

16 See Dunn, *Theology.*

17 Dunn, *Theology,* 53.

18 See Colin E. Gunton, *Christ and Creation,* 1990 Didsbury Lectures (Carlisle, Paternoster, 1993) for a full and cogent development of this theme.

19 Dunn, *Theology,* 53.

20 Dunn, *Theology,* 53.

21 Dunn, *Theology,* 56. See also Robert H. Gundry, *Soma in Biblical Theology, with Emphasis on Pauline Anthropology,* SNTSMS 29 (Cambridge: Cambridge University Press, 1975) and J. A. T. Robinson, *The Body: A Study in Pauline Theology,* SBT 5 (London: SCM, 1952).

22 Dunn, *Theology,* 56.

23 Dunn, *Theology,* 58.

24 André Munzinger, *Discerning the Spirits: Theological and Ethical Hermeneutics in Paul,* SNTSMS 140 (Cambridge: CUP, 2007), 32.

25 Dunn, *Theology,* 58.

26 See Wright, *Romans,* 704.

27 Dunn, *Theology,* 61.

28 See Wright, *Romans,* 592.

29 The NIV which translates *sarx* as 'sinful flesh' in some instances is a case in point.

30 See Robinson, *Body,* 24, who shows that 'flesh' is not inherently evil.

31 Dunn, *Theology,* 73.

32 Dunn, *Theology,* 67.

33 Dunn, *Theology,* 72.

34 Dunn, *Theology,* 73.

35 See John P. Heil, *Ephesians: Empowerment to Walk in Love for the Unity of All in Christ,* Studies in Biblical Literature 13 (Atlanta: Society of Biblical Literature, 2007).

36 Contra Moo, *Romans,* 484.

37 Schreiner, *Romans,* 406.

38 Wright, *Romans,* 578.

39 See Gorman, 'Cruciform', 164.

40 See the challenging article by Diane Leclerc, 'Holiness and Power: Toward a Wesleyan Theology of Dis-Ability', in WTT 44 (2009), 45–69.

41 J. Ross Wagner, 'Working Out Salvation: Holiness and Community in Philippians' in *HENT*, 257–74 (257), citing Morna D. Hooker, 'A Partner in the Gospel: Paul's Understanding of His Ministry', in *Theology and Ethics in Paul and His Interpreters: Essays in Honor of Victor Paul Furnish*, ed. E. H. Lovering, Jr. and J. L. Sumney (Nashville: Abingdon, 1996).

42 Wagner, 'Working Out Salvation', 258.

43 Wagner, 'Working Out Salvation', 264.

44 See L. W. Hurtado, 'Jesus as Lordly Example in Philippians 2:5–11,' in *From Jesus to Paul: Studies in Honour of Francis Wright Beare*, ed. by P. Richardson and J. Hurd (Waterloo: Wilfrid Laurier University Press, 1984), 113–26, who writes 'Jesus' actions are so describe as to present them as a pattern to which the readers are to conform their behaviour' (126).

45 Gorman, 'Cruciform', 161.

46 Wagner, 'Working Out Salvation', 265

47 Wagner, 'Working Out Salvation', 265.

48 Gorman, 'Cruciform', 162.

49 Hays, 'The Role of Scripture', 37.

50 See Heil, *Ephesians*.

51 Wright, *Romans*, 580.

52 Fee, *Empowering Presence*, 537.

53 Dunn, *Theology*, 75.

54 See, for instance, Moo, *Romans*, 743.

55 See Munzinger, *Discerning the Spirits*, 40.

56 Munzinger, *Discerning the Spirits*, 40–41.

57 Munzinger, *Discerning the Spirits*, 193.

58 Dunn, *Theology*, 74.

59 Contra Moo, *Romans*, 757, who reads it as 'so that you can approve', a purpose clause rather than a result clause.

60 It may only be coincidental that Paul uses *teleios* here to describe the will of God; the cognate *telos* is used when Christ is the 'fulfilment of the law' in 10:4.

61 William M. Greathouse, *Romans 9—16: A Commentary in the Wesleyan Tradition*. NBBC (Kansas City: Beacon Hill, 2008), 137.

62 See Dunn, *Theology*, 669.

63 Moo, *Romans*, 756–57 cited by Greathouse, *Romans 9—16*, 137.

64 Greathouse, *Romans 9—16*, 137.

65 Robert Jewett, *Romans: A Commentary*, Hermeneia: A Critical and Historical Commentary on the Bible (Minneapolis: Fortress, an imprint of Augsburg Fortress, 2007), 524.

66 Jewett, *Romans*, 526.

67 For full discussion see Cranfield, *Romans. Vol. 1*, 424–31. See also Jewett (*Romans*, 526–28), who reaches different conclusions from Cranfield.

68 Jewett, *Romans*, 525–26.

69 Wright, *Romans*, 706.

70 Wright, *Romans*, 541.

71 See John Wesley's two sermons of 'The Witness of the Spirit'.

72 See Wright, *Romans*, 593.

73 Jewett, *Romans*, 498.

74 Jewett, *Romans*, 500.

75 So Dunn, *Romans*, 457; Moo, *Romans*, 505.

76 See Jewett, *Romans*, 503.

77 Contra Greathouse, *Romans 9—16*, 217.

78 So Wright, *Romans*, 741.

79 See Donald P. Mentch, 'Righteousness, Peace and Joy in the Holy Spirit: Holiness and Ethics in Paul's Epistle to the Romans', (MA dissertation, Nazarene Theological College, 1998) for a discussion that shows how sectors of the holiness movement have confused holiness with micro-ethics while missing the heart of Paul's description of the holy people.

80 Fee, *God's Empowering Presence*, 476.

81 Jewett, *Romans*, 525.

82 Wright, *Romans*, 599.

83 See Fee, *God's Empowering Presence*, 79.

84 Fee, *God's Empowering Presence*, 79.

85 See David G. Peterson, *Possessed by God: A New Testament Theology of Sanctification and Holiness*, New Studies in Biblical Theology (Leicester: Apollos/IVP, 1995), 60–62.

86 In fact, this is all part of Paul's re-reading of Isaiah 66:20 in the light of Christ.

87 See Greathouse, *Romans 9—16*, 244.

88 Oakes, 'Romans', 169.

89 Jewett, *Romans*, 908.

90 Jewett, *Romans*, 907.

91 Greathouse, *Romans 9—16*.

92 Wagner, 'Working out Salvation', 264.

93 J. D. G. Dunn, *The Theology of Paul's Letter to the Galatians. NTT.* (Cambridge: Cambridge University Press, 1993), 62.

94 Dunn, *Theology of Galatians*, 62.

95 James D. G. Dunn, ' "The Law of Faith," "the Law of the Spirit" and "the Law of Christ" ', in *Theology and Ethics in Paul and his Interpreters: Essays in Honor of Victor Paul Furnish*, ed. Eugene H. Lovering, Jr. and Jerry L. Sumney (Nashville: Abingdon, 1996), 62–82 (70–71).

96 J. A. Ziesler, *The Epistle to the Galatians* (London: Epworth, 1992), 79.

97 Gorman, 'Cruciform', 157.

98 See A. C. Thiselton, *The First Epistle to the Corinthians*, The New International Greek Testament Commentary (Carlisle: Paternoster, 2000), 17, who suggests that the context in Corinthians 'provides an embarrassingly close model of a postmodern context for the gospel in our own times.'

99 J. Paul Sampley, *The First Letter to the Corinthians* in *The New Interpreter's Bible*, Vol X (Nashville: Abingdon, 2002), 944.

100 Gorman, 'Cruciform', 152.

101 Paul Kariuki Njiru, *Charisms and the Holy Spirit's Activity in the Body of Christ: An Exegetical-Theological Study of 1 Corinthians 12, 4–11 and Romans 12, 6–8* (Tesi Gregoriana: Serie Teologia 86; Roma: Editrice Pontificia Universita Gregoriana, 2002), 184.

102 Njiru, *Charisma*, 9.

103 Munzinger, *Discerning the Spirits*, 195.

104 Sampley, *Corinthians*, 943.

Chapter Three: Holiness and Community in Corinth

1 See David G. Horrell, *The Social Ethos of the Corinthian Correspondence* (Edinburgh: T&T Clark, 1996) for a detailed survey of recent work; see also Thiselton, *1 Corinthians*, 25–27, 183.

2 Sampley, *Corinthians*, 814.

3 Ben Witherington, III, *Conflict and Community in Corinth* (Carlisle: Paternoster, 1995), 24.

4 Witherington, *Corinth*, 20.

5 Bruce Winter, 'Carnal Conduct and Sanctification in 1 Corinthians: *simul sanctus et peccator?*' in *HENT*, 186, who cites the fourth century B.C. plays of Philetaerus 13.559a and Poliochus, 7.31.3 'The Whoremonger ὁ Κορινθιαστής)' and Plato, *The Republic*, 404C in which a 'Corinthian girl' = a prostitute.

6 Winter, 'Carnal', 186 n. 4.

7 See Margaret Y. MacDonald, 'Slavery, Sexuality and House Churches: A Reassessment of Colossians 3.18–4.1 in Light of New Research on the Roman Family', in *NTS* 53 (2007), 94–113.

8 Gorman, 'Cruciform', 165, citing Dunn, *Theology*, 690.

9 Gorman, 'Cruciform', 165.

10 Andy Johnson, 'The Sanctification of the Imagination in 1 Thessalonians', *HENT*, 275–92 (287).

11 Winter, 'Carnal', 186.

12 See Roy E. Ciampa and Brian S. Rosner, 'The Structure and Argument of 1 Corinthians: A Biblical/Jewish Approach', *NTS* 52 (2006), 205–18 who argue that the whole epistle is built around the theme of purity.

13 This section summaries part of the discussion in Brower, *Holiness in the Gospels*, 21–29. See references to further the literature in this book.

14 Hurtado, *Origins*, 12.

15 Hurtado, *Origins*, 21.

16 See Hannah Harrington, *Holiness: Rabbinic Judaism and the Graeco-Roman World* (London/New York: Routledge, 2001).

17 Witherington, *Corinth*, 13.

18 See G. I. Davies, 'The Presence of God in the Second Temple and Rabbinic Doctrine', *Templum Amicitiae*, ed. W. Horbury, JSNTSS 48 (Sheffield: JSOT, 1991), 33, who writes, 'belief in the divine presence in the Second Temple was much more widespread than is commonly allowed.'

19 See Kent Brower, 'The Holy One and his Disciples': Holiness and Ecclesiology in Mark', *HENT*, 57–75.

20 Thiselton, *1 Corinthians*, 307.

21 See Thiselton, *1 Corinthians*, 315.

22 Sampley, *Corinthians*, 831. The other usages by Paul confirm the possibility of this semantic range.

23 A similar idea might be present in 1 Cor. 11:29–34.

24 See the helpful discussion in Sampley, 864.

25 Sampley, *Corinthians*, 860–61, reminds us that Paul does not reject the slogan, although he tellingly removes 'for me'.

26 See Macdonald, 'Slavery, Sexuality and House Churches'. Macdonald shows the extent to which slaves were used for sexual purposes within the Graeco-Roman context, and drawing attention to the counter-cultural perspective of Christians at this point as well.

27 This next paragraph is an abridgement drawn from Winter, 'Carnal'.

28 Winter cites A. Booth, 'The Age for Reclining and its Attendant Perils' in W. J. Slater ed., *Dining in a Classical Context* (Ann Arbor: University of Michigan Press, 1991), 105, ' "The intimate and unholy trinity" of eating, drinking and sexual immorality.'

29 Winter writes, 'The young Corinthian men would have subscribed to the inscription on a sculpture of a phallic symbol now in the Archaeological Museum, Naples—'here dwells happiness' (*hic habitat felicitas*). See C. Mills and J. J. Norwich, *Love in the Ancient World* (London: Orion, 1997), 125.

30 Alistair Scott May, *'The Body for the Lord': Sex and Identity in 1 Corinthians 5—7*, JSNTSS 278 (London: T&T Clark International, an imprint of Continuum, 2004), 266.

31 May, *Body*, 266.

32 Christine E. Hayes, *Gentile Impurities and Jewish Identities: Intermarriage and Conversion from the Bible to the Talmud* (Oxford: Oxford University Press, 2002), 103.

33 The theological roots for this belief may depend upon the social image of the triune God reflected in the relationship between man and woman, but if so, Paul doesn't develop the thought.

34 Thiselton, *1 Corinthians*, 468, cites Dale Martin, *The Corinthian Body* (New Haven: Yale, 1995), 176, 'The man who has sex with a prostitute is, in Paul's construction, Christ's "member" entering the body of the prostitute.'

35 Sampley, *Corinthians*, 865.

36 See Ciampa and Rosner, '1 Corinthians', 205–18.

37 Jeffrey A. D. Weima, ' "How you must walk to please God": Holiness and Discipleship in 1 Thessalonians' in *Patterns of Discipleship in the New Testament*, ed. Richard N. Longenecker (McMaster New Testament Studies; Grand Rapids: Eerdmans, 1996): 98–121 (111–112).

38 See Ciampa and Rosner, '1 Corinthians'. See also Sarah K. Whittle, '2 Corinthians 6:14 – 7:1 "Come Out From Among Them!" Calling the Corinthians to Covenant Holiness', MA thesis, University of Manchester 2007.
39 Weima, 'Walk' 103.
40 See Johnson, 'Sanctification of the Imagination', *HENT,* 276–78 for the same theme in I Thessalonians.
41 Thiselton, *1 Corinthians*, 725, italics original.
42 Thiselton, *1 Corinthians*, 725.
43 See Excursus in Thiselton, *1 Corinthians*, 727–30.
44 Witherington, *Corinth*, 218.
45 See Witherington, *Corinth*, 218 and Thiselton, *1 Corinthians*, 727–30.
46 See Bruce Fish, 'Pseudo-Philo, Paul and Israel's Rolling Stone: Early Points along an Exegetical Trajectory', *Israel in the Wilderness: Interpretations of the Biblical Narratives in the Jewish and Christian Traditions.* Themes in Biblical Narrative: Jewish and Christian Traditions 10, ed. Kenneth E. Pomykala (Leiden/ Boston: Brill, 2008), 117–36.
47 See John I. Dunham, *Exodus*, WBC 3 (Waco: Word, 1987), 422, who notes the sexual connotations of the word translated 'revel'. B. S. Childs, *The Book of Exodus*, OTL (Philadelphia: Westminster, 1974), 566 comments, 'A religious orgy has begun.'
48 Thiselton, *1 Corinthians*, 735.
49 See Winter, 'Carnal', 188.
50 Thiselton, *1 Corinthians*, 735.
51 See Johnson, 'Sanctification of the Imagination'.
52 Fee, *I Corinthians*, 532.
53 See J. D. G. Dunn, *I Corinthians*, NTG (Sheffield: SAP, 1995), 78.
54 Interestingly enough, although Paul 'getting drunk' at the table would have been appalling to Paul (cf. Eph 5:18), his concern is that some people go hungry (11:21).
55 Dunn, *I Corinthians*, 78.
56 See Sampley, *Corinthians* 938.
57 The variant readings in 11:29 are interesting. The earliest witnesses, including $\mathfrak{P}^{46}$ and $\aleph^*$ read γὰρ ἐσθίων καὶ πίνων κρίμα ἑαυτῷ ἐσθίει καὶ πίνει μὴ διακρίνων τὸ σῶμα. A longer version represented by the Western text and most MSS adds adds ἀναξίως after πίνων and τοῦ κυρίου after τὸ σῶμα. While the shorter reading is to be preferred, this variant may suggest that

fairly early in the transmission of the text, scribes decided to clarify that the body in question was Jesus, and not the church. This point was drawn to my attention by my colleague, Dr. D. Swanson.

58 Thiselton, *1 Corinthians*, 889, italics original.

59 Sampley, *Corinthians* 934.

60 Dunn, *1 Corinthians*, 78.

61 Vincent Taylor, *Jesus and His Sacrifice: A Study of the Passion Sayings of the Gospels* (London: Macmillan, 1937), 212.

62 The issue is essentially hermeneutical. See Willard Swartley, *Slavery, Sabbath, War and Women: Case Issues in Biblical Interpretation* (Scottsdale: Herald Press, 1987) for a helpful discussion of hermeneutical principles. The debate about the role and place of women in leadership is established in principle in the holiness movement denominations. In practice, the issue still bubbles beneath the surface. For a useful discussion see R. T. France, *Women in Ministry: A test case for biblical interpretation*, The 1995 Didsbury Lectures (Carlisle: Paternoster, 1997).

63 Fee, *First Epistle to the Corinthians*, NICNT (Grand Rapids: Eerdmans, 1995), 544.

64 Indeed, Robert Banks, in *Paul's Idea of Community* (Peabody: Hendrickson, 1994, 2nd edition, 135), argues that 'Paul has no place in his view of the community for the traditional distinctions between its members along cultic, official or religious lines.'

65 Thiselton, *1 Corinthians*, 1145.

66 See Dean Flemming, 'On Earth as It Is in Heaven': Holiness and the People of God in Revelation', *HENT*, 343–62. Flemming shows that teachers in the community (Rev. 2:15; 2:20–23) 'apparently encouraged accommodation as a way of surviving in the Roman world. Revelation calls for separation from such "normal" cultural practices. Through John's prophetic eyes, they represent a syncretistic collusion with state-sponsored idolatry. Revelation reinforces the need for God's people to be a countercultural community' (353).

67 Deasley, *The Shape of Qumran Theology*, 238. This is seen particularly in the 4Q*ShirShabb* texts, 'Songs of the Sabbath Sacrifice'. The texts below are all cited by Deasley, 239.

68 This is not a new idea. Henry J. Cadbury, in 'A Qumran Parallel to Paul' (*Harvard Theological Review* 51 (1958), 1–2), already

drew it attention to it. Since then the publication of other Qumran MSS has added significantly to the point.

69 Thiselton, *1 Corinthians*, 843, thinks that the angels are understood by Paul to be the guardians of order.

70 Recent commentators, such as Richard B. Hays, *First Corinthians, Interpretation* (Louisville: John Knox, 1997), 188, quite rightly reject the traditional interpretation that this is connected to Genesis 6:1–4.

71 See the excellent discussion in Francis Watson, 'The Authority of the Voice: A Theological Reading of 1 Cor. 11:2—16', *NTS* 46 (2000), 520–36.

72 See Francis Watson. *Agape, Eros, Gender: Towards a Pauline Sexual Ethic* (Cambridge, Cambridge University Press: 2000) for extensive background discussion.

73 See K. E. Brower, 'Jesus and the Lustful Eye: Glancing at Matthew 5:28', *Evangelical Quarterly*, 76 (2004), 291–309.

74 George J. Brooke, 'From Qumran to Corinth: Embroidered Allusions to Women's Authority', *The Dead Sea Scrolls and the New Testament* (London/Philadephia: SPCK/Fortress, 2005): 195–214.

75 Brooke, 'Qumran to Corinth', 206.

76 Brooke, 'Qumran to Corinth', 206.

77 Brooke, 'Qumran to Corinth', 206.

78 Brooke, 'Qumran to Corinth', 213.

79 Brooke, 'Qumran to Corinth', 214.

80 See Bruce Winter, *Seek the Welfare of the City: Christians as Benefactors and Citizens* (Carlisle: Paternoster, 1994), 105–21.

81 Fee, *1 Corinthians*, 100.

82 See John M. G. Barclay, *Obeying the Truth: A Study of Paul's Ethics in Galatians*, Studies of the New Testament and its World, ed. John Riches (Edinburgh: T&T Clark, 1988), 146–154.

83 Barclay, *Obeying*, 157.

84 Barclay, *Obeying*, 157.

85 J. Louis Martyn, *Galatians*, AB 33A (New York/London: Doubleday, 1997), 546.

86 J. D. G. Dunn, *The Epistle to the Galatians*, BNTC (Peabody: Hendrickson, 1993), 319–20, offers a range of possibilities before narrowing it to this suggestion.

87 The interpretation of this passage presents numerous challenges. The full discussion in Thiselton, *I Corinthians*, 382–400 is thorough, cogent and persuasive.

88 J. Ayodeji Adwuya, 'The People of God in a Pluralistic Society: Holiness in 2 Corinthians', *HENT*, 201–18 (216).
89 Thiselton, *1 Corinthians*, 17, italics original.

Chapter Four: Holiness in the Real World

1 See Greg K. Beale, 'The Eschatological Conception of New Testament Theology' in *'The Reader Must Understand': Eschatology in Bible and Theology*, ed by K. E. Brower and M. W. Elliott, Apollos (Leicester: Apollos, IVP, 1997, 31–52 for an important article highlighting the importance of this concept for New Testament theology.
2 Dunn, *Theology*, 411.
3 Campbell, *Identity*, 165.
4 Campbell, *Identity*, 93, italics original.
5 The authorship of Ephesians is in dispute. See F. F. Bruce who calls it 'the Quintessence of Paulinism' in *Paul: Apostle of the Free Spirit* (Exeter: Paternoster, 1977), 424.
6 Beale, 'Eschatological Conception', 35.
7 See Moyer V. Hubbard, *New Creation in Paul's Letters and Thought*, SNTSMS 119 (Cambridge: Cambridge University Press, 2002).
8 Hubbard, *New Creation*, 238.
9 Beale, 32.
10 Ben Witherington, III, *Paul's Narrative Thought World: The Tapestry of Tragedy and Triumph* (Louisville: John Knox/Westminster, 1994), 274.
11 Hubbard, *New Creation*, 232.
12 Hubbard, *New Creation*, 235.
13 Hubbard, *New Creation*, 235, his italics.
14 Hubbard, *New Creation*, 235.
15 Witherington, *Paul's Narrative Thought World*, 274.
16 See Witherington, *Paul's Narrative Thought World*, 274.
17 T. Ware, *The Orthodox Church* (Harmondsworth: Penguin, 1993, revised edn), 209.
18 See David Horrell, Cherryl Hunt, Christopher Southgate, 'Appeals to the Bible in Ecotheology and Environmental Ethics: a Typology of Hermeneutical Stances', *Studies in Christian Ethics* 21 (2008), 219–38.

19 This view is usually aligned with a premillennial interpretation of New Testament eschatology and depends upon a particular interpretation of passages like 2 Peter 3:10; Rev. 20:4–6.

20 Jewett, *Romans*, 512.

21 Dunn, *Theology*, 403.

22 Brian J. Walsh and Sylvia C. Keesmaat, *Colossians Remixed: Subverting the Empire* (Carlisle: Paternoster, 2004), 173.

23 Dunn, *Theology*, 411.

24 As has been demonstrated by grammarians, the aorist passive as used here by Paul [*hupetagē*] is better understood to refer to a repeated action, rather than a once off occurrence in the past. Contra J. Moo, 'Romans 8:19–22', 78 who thinks it points to a particular past event.

25 Laurie Braaten, 'All Creation Groans: Romans 8:22 in Light of the Biblical Sources' in *Horizons in Biblical Theology* 28 (2006), 131–59.

26 Nwachukwu, *Creation-Covenant Scheme* 250.

27 Jewett, *Romans*, 512.

28 Wright, *Romans*, 605.

29 Wright, *Romans*, 606.

30 For details, see Peter Oakes, *Philippians: From People to Letter*, SNTSMS 110 (Cambridge: Cambridge University Press, 2001). For Roman citizenship, see also A. N. Sherwin-White, *Roman Citizenship* (Oxford: Oxford University Press, 1973); Winter, *Seek the Welfare of the City*; Brian Rapske, *The Book of Acts and Paul in Roman Custody* in The Book of Acts in its First Century Setting, Vol. 3 (Grand Rapids: Eerdmans, 1994).

31 Jewett, *Romans*, 513.

32 Campbell, *Identity*, 83.

33 Campbell, *Identity*, 92.

34 Flemming, 'On Earth', *HENT*, 360.

35 Bockmuehl, *Philippians*, 98.

36 The next section summarizes a section in Gorman, 'Cruciform'. For lengthier discussions of the views presented here, see Gorman, *Cruciformity*, 88–92, 164–69, 278–80, 316–19, and 357–58, as well as the chapter on Philippians in Michael J. Gorman, *Apostle of the Crucified Lord* (Grand Rapids: Eerdmans, 2005), 412–53. For similar interpretations of this text, see Wright, *Climax*, 56–98, and Stephen Fowl, "Christology and Ethics in

Paul," *Where Christology Began: Essays on Philippians 2*, ed. Ralph P. Martin and Brian J. Dodd (Louisville: Westminster John Knox, 1998), 140–53; and *The Story of Christ in the Ethics of Paul*, JSNTSS 36 (Sheffield: JSOT Press, 1990), 49–101.

37 Gorman, 'Cruciform', 160, with supporting evidence.

38 Gorman, 'Cruciform', 160. For a fuller discussion of Paul's notion of a kenotic or cruciform God, see Gorman, *Cruciformity*, 9–18.

39 Gorman, *Cruciformity*, 169.

40 Wagner, 'Working out Salvation', 266.

41 Campbell, *Identity*, 36.

42 Gorman, 'Cruciform', 162.

43 Bockmuehl, *Philippians*, 217.

44 Wagner, 'Working out Salvation', 268.

45 Wagner, 'Working out Salvation', 258.

46 See K. E. Brower, 'Eschatology', *New Dictionary of Biblical Theology* (Leicester: IVP, 2000).

47 See, in particular, the three volumes by J. C. Beker, *Paul the Apostle* (Philadelphia: Fortress, 1980), *Paul's Apocalyptic Gospel* (Philadelphia: Fortress, 1985) and *The Triumph of God*. See also Käsemann, *Romans*, Wright, *Climax*, and Dunn, *Theology*.

48 Richard B. Hays, 'Christ Died for the Ungodly: Narrative Soteriology in Paul?' (paper for the SBL Pauline Soteriology Ground, Atlanta, 24 November 2003), 7.

49 See the discussion in C. A. Wanamaker, *Commentary on 1 & 2 Thessalonians*, NIGNTC (Grand Rapids/Exeter: Eerdmans/Paternoster, 1990), 10–16.

50 Wanamaker, *Thessalonians*, 10.

51 Johnson, 'Sanctification of the Imagination', 278.

52 Morna D. Hooker, 'A Partner in the Gospel', 99.

53 L. Ann Jervis, 'Becoming like God through Christ: Discipleship in Romans' in *Patterns of Discipleship in the New Testament*, ed. Richard N. Longenecker (McMaster New Testament Studies; Grand Rapids: Eerdmans, 1996), 143–162 (161).

54 Marshall, *1 & 2 Thessalonians* 72, emphasis original.

55 E. Best, *The First and Second Epistles to the Thessalonians*, BNTC (London/Peabody: A & C Black/Hendrickson, 1972), 151.

56 See K. E. Brower, '1 Thessalonians', *Asbury Bible Commentary* (Grand Rapids: Zondervan, 1992), 1099.

57 Johnson, 'Sanctification of the Imagination', 284.

58 Idem.

59 Brower, *ABC*, 1100. No doubt Paul was very aware of the prominence given in Thessalonica to the Cabiri cults with their accompanying sexual immorality. See F. F. Bruce, *1 and 2 Thessalonians*, WBC (Waco: Word, 1982), 82.

60 Note the distinction between 'to impurity' and 'in holiness'. See Johnson, 'Sanctification', 287.

61 Bruce, *Thessalonians*, 72.

62 Schreiner, *Paul* 222, writes 'God will sanctify his people completely at the coming of Jesus Christ ... The God who called his people to salvation will surely complete the sanctifying work he has begun. The future holiness of believers is assured because it depends upon God himself.'

63 Bruce, *Thessalonians*, 72.

64 Brower, '1 Thessalonians', 1100.

65 Best, *Thessalonians*, 243.

66 Bruce, *Thessalonians*, 131.

67 Best, *Thessalonians*, 242.

68 Sampley, *Corinthians*, 846.

69 See Brian S. Rosner, *Paul's Scripture and Ethics: A Study of I Corinthians 5–7*, Arbeiten Zur Geschichte Des Antiken Judentums und Des Urchristentums (Tübingen: J C B Mohr, 1994).

70 But far more than is sometimes thought. See David Wenham, *Paul: Follower of Jesus or Founder of Christianity?* (Grand Rapids: Eerdmans, 1995).

71 Sampley, *Corinthians*, 877.